Juliano Pimentel
FOREWORD **JOEL JOTA**

Anxiety

Distributed in English language by:

SOUND WISDOM

P.O. Box 310 • Shippensburg, PA 17257-0310 • 717-530-2122

info@soundwisdom.com

DISCLAIMER

The information available in this book does not under any circumstances replace professional medical advice. The author and publisher bear no responsibility for how the information contained herein is used by the reader. Therefore, the reader should always consult their doctor on any matter relating to their health and the treatments and medicines they use.

Juliano Pimentel
FOREWORD **JOEL JOTA**

Anxiety

MASTER YOUR MIND.
LIVE WITHOUT FEAR.

2024

CONTENTS

PREFACE 7

FOREWORD 11

INTRODUCTION 15

CHAPTER 1 21

CHAPTER 2 61

CHAPTER 3 79

CHAPTER 4 107

CHAPTER 5 133

CHAPTER 6 155

CHAPTER 7 177

CHAPTER 8 205

EPILOGUE 227

REFERENCES 235

PREFACE

Writing a foreword is always a double-edged activity for me: responsibility and pride. Writing the one for this book, in particular, has a third element: a life principle. And why do I say that? Because it's a book that deals with issues of great importance in our lives, but above all it's a work about health.

I have and follow a philosophy: "Health, family and work, don't reverse the order". For a few years of my life I put work first, and the results, in the medium term, weren't the way I wanted them to be. This happened after my career as a professional swimmer came to an end. I focused only on work, put on 22 kilos, developed cellular inflammation and even a cancerous nodule appeared on my thyroid. It was mental, emotional and physical hell. And believe it or not, all this with a former Brazilian national team athlete and master in sports science. In other words, I wasn't spared because nobody is. If we neglect the greatest of all our assets, which is our health, we will be doomed to all the consequences that this can bring to any of us.

Therefore, to begin to describe the importance of a work like this carries significant weight for me, but above all for the readers who will gain an in-depth understanding of the benefits, harms and consequences of healthy and unhealthy living.

Dr. Juliano is the right person to deal with this issue, but don't expect him to be neutral in his words and subtle with you. No, he won't. Juliano knows what he's talking about, how he's talking about it, who he's talking to and, above all, what he believes in. From his career as a health professional to his life experiences that further reinforce what he believes. He will treat you like an adult.

Here's another of his many contributions. If you turn on his Instagram profile in the morning, while you're having breakfast, getting ready for work or perhaps changing your child for school, you can have a lesson in mental, physical, cognitive and spiritual health with him. Every day he's there, focused, generous and touching many people's wounds with a single purpose: healing.

I've already had the opportunity to do a few lives with him, attend lectures and share stages alongside him, and I can say with certainty: Dr. Juliano will provoke you, question you, cause you concern, and it will work. This is the method he will use to ensure that you understand in the following pages that our mind, without the connection to our body, can make us sick for a lifetime. That our essence is so wise, but that our thoughts can stifle it, and even cause physical illnesses that we will carry with us for the rest of our lives. And that has to stop!

We have the power and ability to change our reality and our surroundings through the thoughts and feelings we create, and in this book you'll learn how to do it for good. There are countless reflections and lessons to be learned. It will be quite a journey into the world of health, with an eye on a subject that needs to be dealt with carefully: anxiety.

The world is becoming increasingly anxious. Brazil is one of the countries that suffers most from anxiety and depression in the world. You see, it affects everyone, and many people, believe me, don't even know they suffer from it. When I saw the greatest athlete in the history of the Olympic Games, swimmer Michael Phelps, admit that he had suffered from severe depression for years, I stopped to reflect deeply: "Well, if Phelps has and acknowledges that depression has been present in his life, imagine for us mere mortals?". This subject is so strong that phrases like "It's ok not to be ok" have circulated in the sports world. And when we think of these champions, we imagine armored, impenetrable minds. Well, it's not like that, it doesn't work that way. And today there is a worldwide concern to learn how to deal with anxiety and depression.

This book is another one of those powerful tools that is now in your hands. And you'll notice over the next few pages that it's not just for you. The urge to explain and even give someone a copy of this book will recur. And the reason is simple: we are here to serve each other. It's human nature to do so.

Enjoy the journey, take another step towards understanding yourself and become even healthier. You're in great hands. A big hug and have a good flight.

– Joel Jota

PRESENTATION

WHO HAS BEEN RULING YOUR MIND, YOURSELF OR YOUR ANXIETY?

Despite being a natural and fundamental condition in the history of human construction, anxiety has long since ceased to be part of an instinctive physiological system of action to occupy the body, mind and soul of a large part of humanity.

But what has changed since then to stop a growing number of people living their lives to the full, becoming increasingly hostage to fear, anxiety and depression?

In Anxiety: the end of slavery, you'll finally understand why you live as a slave to your mind, which insists on being disconnected from your body; why you feel that your energy is being drained throughout the day; why you fall ill even when you're sure you're doing everything you can to avoid becoming ill.

If you've come to this book, it's likely that you've felt anxious at some point in your life. To a certain extent, this is natural and to be expected, especially since anxiety, to a certain degree, is beneficial in the sense that it generates productive movement in the individual's life. But have you ever stopped to analyze what is considered acceptable from a health point of view?

Not to mention the agitation, fatigue and sense of frustration and helplessness in the face of a world increasingly collapsed by threats such as the pandemic that has caught us by surprise.

INTRODUCTION

IT'S NOT "WHY?". IT'S "WHAT FOR"

It had been five years since Carol and I had said goodbye to contraceptive methods, and we thought that if a baby was to come, it would come at the best time. We were at the peak of our health, she having lost more than 40 kilos since joining the weight loss method I created especially for her, so that we could get married the way she dreamed of. We continued to work together and were increasingly fulfilled by helping tens of thousands of people to take full care of their health.

One morning, with my period late, the long-awaited positive result arrived. It was the end of 2019, and this "positive" was much celebrated. But what no one imagined was that, in the aftermath, we would all face the global outbreak of Covid-19. And for us, the worst hadn't even arrived yet...

Despite being in excellent health, Carol faced many body reactions during her pregnancy. An unbearable and widespread itch began to accompany her, to the point where doctors diagnosed her with scabies. So many sleepless nights.

At eight months pregnant, my wife had to deal with a few scares because of my father-in-law's health, who had high blood pressure spikes and needed medical help three times. She also had to worry about the health of our dog, who almost went blind in one eye, and so on... One challenge after another.

Even with everything converging to make her more and more anxious about a pregnancy that wasn't going smoothly, in the midst of endless quarantine and the intermittent threat of an unknown virus, Carol stood her ground. She wasn't afraid, she didn't sink into anxiety.

But what about when a "death sentence" arrives?

* * *

About a month after giving birth, our baby needed supplementation because she couldn't suckle. In addition, Carol's breasts still felt very strange. From the very first feeding in the maternity ward, we noticed a large lump in her left breast, and everyone said it must be milk. You know that famous woman's intuition? As she noticed that the lump wasn't going away, one day, at the end of a feed, she asked me to check again, this time with the breast completely emptied.

I remember it as if it were today! A week earlier, I had felt in my heart that I should intensify my prayers. As soon as I touched her breast, I looked straight into her eyes, already sensing that something wasn't right. I began to understand the reason for those feelings. Right away, with her eyes watering, she said: "I'm going to fast!".

From that day on, everything went very quickly. Carol underwent an ultrasound that showed a very strange image, and right there the doctor biopsied her and took the sample to the laboratory. Meanwhile, I called our friend, Dr. Raphael Brandão, and the next day we went to São Paulo for a consultation and a battery of tests.

When Carol opened that envelope, the world fell apart. The feeling was that there was no longer any ground beneath our feet. That was the first reaction we had when we were diagnosed with breast cancer, a month after our daughter was born. It was a seven-centimeter tumor, which immediately made her think that she was going to die and leave our family alone, leave our one-month-old baby for me to take care of alone.

In a situation like this, all the adrenaline in the body goes off automatically. There's no room for the control of our adrenal glands, so everything is affected. Inevitably, the breathing, the cognitive system, the sweating, the palpitations, the cold in the belly and the tremors all appear. There is only room for an overwhelming anxiety that insists on throwing us into a future moment that exists only in our mind and nowhere else.

Uncertainty reared its head. The feeling was one of despair and helplessness. That day, we were faced with chaos. While Carol was screaming "Why, God? Why, my God?", already dismounted on the floor, I spent fifteen seconds in a deep panic, which seemed like hours. But when the shock wore off, like a bolt of lightning that pierced me through the middle, I came to my wife's aid and, overwhelmed by the peace that transcends understanding, I took her by the hand and said: "It's not why? What for?

* * *

There are many challenging moments in our lives. They can come in the form of a major change that comes our way, such as a loss, a separation, an illness or a host of other "fears" that arise within us. But the big question is: how do you react to life's events?

If your answer is to fill yourself with worries that take away your sleep, affect your performance, completely change your routine and ruin your health, then yes, you are another anxious or pathologically anxious person.

However, if you dedicate yourself carefully to reading and completing each of the exercises proposed in this book, you will not only learn to identify and defuse the potentially dangerous triggers of the most varied anxiety conditions, but you will also change your response to anxiety forever.

In the following chapters, you'll see how anxiety as we know it was built, which fears feed it and make it stronger, discover the differences between anxiety and depression, how your immunity is affected by anxiety, whether medication is the solution and, above all, learn the rules of the game so that you can change it yourself and thus transform your life, as Carol and I did in this battle against cancer and in many others.

A CONSTRUCTION BASED ON FEAR

In fact, God has not given us a spirit of fear, but a spirit of strength, love and wisdom

(2 Tm 1:7)

Anxiety is part of the construction of human history. We've only got this far because anxiety has played a part in our evolution. In this context, just as people say that obesity is closely related to natural selection, anxiety also plays a role in this story. But why, after all?

A QUESTION OF SURVIVAL

To understand anxiety, let's go back to the beginning. In the early days of human civilization, in order for a person to protect themselves from dangers, such as a predator attack, they had to anticipate what might happen and then build a trap to keep their life safe. This "concern" was a matter of care. However, at the same time as foreseeing the dangers, she couldn't remain paralyzed; after all, she had to act on them. It was a question of survival.

Back then, this was done naturally by our ancestors, it was healthy and intermittent. But what happens now, in this day and age, is quite different. Today, people are trapped in a context of anxiety because they have placed all their trust in everything that happens in the external world. This gradual distancing from our essence has worsened as society has evolved, from an industrial and technological point of view, but has regressed in terms of behavior, especially with regard to itself, in other words, in the field of self-knowledge.

Want a simple example? Breathing. What we see most today is the inability of many people to simply breathe properly. They have lost this natural and intrinsic resource, that is, one that is inherent to our being, which allows them to change their physical and mental pattern in the face of a stressful situation, and have started to make room for compulsive thinking, automatic actions and persistence in anticipating the unknown, lulled by a speed that is increasingly sold as a benefit by the world around them.

Every life begins with an act of breathing in, followed by a loud cry. However, when we talk about breathing, we need to look at another point: with every breath we take, we get closer to death, just as every day could be our last. And, as you'll discover later, one of the most aggravated forms of anxiety is related to one of our greatest fears: death.

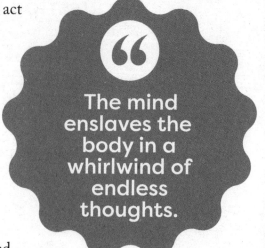

> The mind enslaves the body in a whirlwind of endless thoughts.

Now, if you're wondering what role fear plays in anxiety, I can tell you that the two are almost always closely linked.

The shadow of fear

What do you feel when you are afraid? Reactionary patterns such as tachycardia, body chills, excessive sweating and shortness of breath are usually the most common. Now, try to remember an event in which you found yourself in a state of extreme anxiety. It's likely that you experienced these same reactions and even others discharged through the body. This is basically because the origin of pathological anxiety lies in our main fears, which in turn are instinctive, linked to the most primitive side of our mind, which has always been part of us.

Being anxious beyond what is considered natural is the same as living in the shadow of fear. Fear itself is a defense mechanism, just like natural anxiety. Its primary function is to guard against dangers that could threaten our existence. Fear prevents us, for example, from exposing ourselves to risks such as walking on a savannah in the midst of hungry lions or eating potentially poisonous berries. Fear has always been responsible for keeping us in a safe zone. However, people have gradually become anxious by remaining trapped in a fertile soil for traps, which is within themselves, called the "mind".

The mental faculties are responsible for managing all our day-to-day functions. Through cognitive processes, we learn more and more about a range of activities, accumulate knowledge and store stories that will form our repertoire. However, this functioning can begin to fail when fear triggers start to emit warnings associated with two specific mental faculties: memory and imagination.

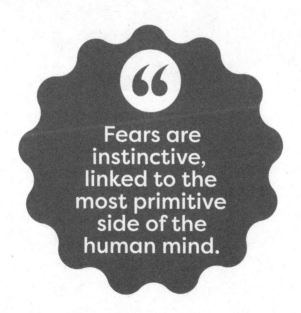

> Fears are instinctive, linked to the most primitive side of the human mind.

Fear, which until then lived in us only as a protective instinct, starts to appear out of the blue, sequestering our mind in a fictitious field of imagination, or even imprisoning our mind in a memory record.

Now, imagine what happens when an individual gets too caught up in an imagination triggered by some traumatic experience. Potentially harmful creations of the mind begin to emerge, and so we have the beginning of anxiety. And when the mind becomes hostage to a memory, even more so a traumatic memory? This condition can trigger depression, which manifests a deep state of disconnection with life.

In an attempt to avoid the fears caused by diving into memory and imagination, people usually look around them for answers to what they are feeling, which they often can't describe. They look for them in the other people around them, in life's circumstances, they distance themselves from themselves at all times and remain that way precisely so that they don't have to look inwards, because this process requires internal changes and sometimes generates pain.

Do you remember the growing pains in your bones? During adolescence, the growth spurt occurs and sometimes children complain of pain in their arms, legs and knees because they are feeling their bones stretching and their muscles developing. If we feel the growing pains in our bodies, why do you think it would be any different when it comes to our minds and spirits?

Is it hard work? Yes! It requires energy, reorganization of habits and daily care, but as long as people don't look inside themselves and face their fears, they will continue to live in a superficial way, facing situations without depth and without genuine answers to their anxieties.

" Growth generates pain. Don't be afraid to feel it.

Anxiety has always been with humanity and is part of a defense mechanism. However, in moments of adversity in life, those of greater tension, there are possibilities in our minds that are not pleasant, because they send us into fear and lead to anxiety.

> **When you don't recognize who you are in the face of some obstacle, fear can appear to be much greater than it really is.**

Once we understand that anxiety and all its derivations originate from exacerbated fears, how can we combat them so that we can begin to detach ourselves from this fear-anxiety circuit? The first step will be to learn to identify them one by one and then know how to deal with them.

Before we go any further, it's important to emphasize that you won't stop feeling fear because, like anxiety, it often acts as a survival mechanism. However, this doesn't mean that you should walk around inconsequentially, nor that you should allow yourself to be paralyzed by fear.

> Fear is just a part of your imagination, and that part can never have power over the whole of you. In other words, you are much bigger than your fear, which is precisely why all the illusory attempts at a gigantic fear that paralyzes your life only take place in your mind. In this way, your shadows, traumas and past memories, which forged the foundation of this fear and make you not recognize who you are in the face of what is holding you back, must fall away.

THE SEVEN MAIN FEARS

As we said at the beginning of this chapter, anxiety is part of our human constitution and has a natural function of preserving the species through our instincts and what we have learned. But when did it stop being something of our nature and become a disease? The answer lies precisely in the fears we decide to embrace and can't let go of.

In my research into what humanity has tried to do to free human beings from the prison of anxiety, I have identified seven fears that I consider to be the main ones in people's lives: fear of rejection, fear of incapacity, fear of illness, fear of humiliation, fear of scarcity, fear of abandonment and fear of death. All of them are capable of triggering the most diverse anxiety conditions when not dealt with properly, and in this book I'll talk about each one and how you can master them, starting with the fear of rejection.

THE FEAR OF REJECTION

How many times in your life have you felt the fear of rejection, that fear of not being accepted? As with many people, my wife Carol's experience of the fear of rejection was no different. The story I'm going to share below was one she experienced when she started communicating with the public on the internet, but take a close look at the path she chose to follow when faced with this first fear.

The power of results

Anxiety, when caused by the fear of rejection, is capable of draining all of a person's genuine power.

Before she became one of the most important digital influencers in the field of health and well-being in Brazil, Carol still had a lot of problems with her self-image. She had reached 103 kilos twice, even after resorting to bariatric surgery. And even though she had lost weight a while later, she was still embarrassed to appear in front of the camera. As soon as I showed Carol the camera, she would stutter, freeze, completely paralyzed. She was afraid of exposing herself, afraid of what other people would think of her, afraid of being "canceled" before she even started her work on the internet.

The fact is that everything I created related to health and weight loss and which has helped hundreds of thousands of people was out of love for her, who wanted to look even more beautiful for our wedding. So I created a whole method for her to lose the weight she wanted. And when I started building my work on the internet, I realized that I needed my wife by my side.

At the time, he said to Carol: "My love, my social networks are gathering a lot more people who are looking for a pretty face than a professional who can transform their lives. And I need my wife by my side, because her presence will inhibit the creeps".

This process basically consisted of exposing Carol to something very important: our relationship. And that's how she came to the internet.

When I gave her a purpose, namely the maintenance of our relationship, when I asked for her help with something that motivated her in life and vibrated in her heart, it became much bigger than her fear, causing her to build a channel with more than 200,000 people on YouTube and an Instagram with more than 300,000 people, helping hundreds of thousands of women with her work.

By combating the fear of rejection evidenced by her initial apprehension in front of the cameras, she had finally begun to close wounds that had been open for a long time because of her past. But it was all a process. A process of acceptance, freeing herself from the fear of rejection, of letting go of the past, so that she could finally blossom into who she truly was. Carol hadn't known herself until then. So much so that, in one of our only two fights in our lives, she said: "Why are you with me? Why don't you break up?". I replied simply: "Because I've fallen in love with the woman you don't even know you are. Some time later, and already living fully, Carol was able to tell me that I had saved her in so many ways that she couldn't even conceive of.

Love, which heals everything, made her overcome the first great fear that paralyzes many people. Even though she was experiencing the growing pains of the mind and spirit, she moved to be by my side, helping with my projects, without me ever taking the lead in what was essential for her as a human being, so that she could break through her own fears. And then everything unfolded naturally, because satisfactory results came as a result of good work. So there's nothing better than results to see life flow.

"

Healing result! When you set micro-goals and achieve small victories, these achievements generate small results that simply heal.

"

The fear of rejection may seem insurmountable, but that's only a matter of appearance. As with other challenges in life, the important thing is to set micro-goals and focus on achieving them. Micrometas are like the steps on a flight of stairs to be climbed one by one; and, step by step, you will always reach a new level. Each step is a small victory to be celebrated. Then celebrate the flight of stairs you've just conquered, because that is your goal. Finally, after several flights of stairs, you will have reached your goal. When you become aware of each micro-goal that makes up an entire goal, you become clearer about how to achieve your goal.

" Every acceptance generates liberation!

By confronting fear gradually, there will come a point when it naturally dissipates. No wonder God didn't give us a spirit of fear, but of power and love. Carol only freed herself from all that paralyzing feeling and truly became who she was in any environment when she finally understood that, when we look at our past with maturity, every acceptance generates liberation.

But let's look at this question for a moment. Why do people freeze in the face of their fears? Why do they become anxious? Simply because they crave the approval of others when faced with the seemingly dreadful fear of rejection.

Now I ask you: who says you need someone's validation to be accepted? I know that this can often seem strange, but you were already approved even before the creation of the world by the one who knows every hair on your head and every longing in your heart! Now, if God has already approved of you, who can disapprove of you? And what kind of approval are you looking for?

When you free yourself from the need for others' approval and do things from your heart, not worrying about what others will think about what you're doing, you become free of all the shyness and shame that are rooted in fear and its consequent anxiety.

When fear appears, it unleashes a series of manifestations of anxiety in the individual, which, when they cross a fine line, end up making them lose all their power. The person may get results, but if they continue to carry around the anxiety driven by fear, they will never get very far. They could, for example, build a palace so that they will never be called poor again, but they will do so based on the fear of not feeling accepted. In the end, her castle will be a beautiful prison built under the yoke of fear!

Look at what happened during the Covid-19 pandemic. We've all been continually bombarded with catastrophic news, to the point of panic, like when they announced that 1.4 million people would die from the disease in 2021. That really is terrible. But do you know how many people died from fear and anxiety in 2021? Approximately 43 million lives were taken this past year, either naturally or induced by man. However, the overwhelming majority of these cases occurred through the practice of abortion committed by young people driven by anxiety-inducing fear. The number of young people who want to enjoy an adult life without having the competence to bear the consequences of their actions has grown at an alarming rate. However, when a society becomes so sick with fear that it keeps people increasingly anxious and unprepared to face life's adversities and raise children, even protecting them from dangers and atrocities, the result is unfortunately death. When in your life have you heard someone talk about abortion related to anxiety?

Anxiety really is a thief of our today, which makes us lose tomorrow by simply projecting us from the now into a negative future. That's how it takes us away from the only place that would give us answers, which is our present.

LEARN TO FACE YOUR MONSTERS

Since anxiety in its harmful form is triggered by our fears, we need to understand that it begins to run silently along the edges of our subconscious until it takes over our conscious attitudes. Think, for example, of the impulses that sometimes strike you. It could be an uncontrollable urge to eat a sweet or drink a certain beverage because you think that momentary comfort will solve some problem you're going through, or that excessive worry that comes close to bedtime because you're sure you won't be able to sleep because it's happened before. In all these situations, you don't even realize that you've already been taken over by the controls of anxiety, projecting yourself into fantasies of your imagination set in a future you haven't lived yet or dragging yourself through memories of the past. And so anxiety continues to displace you from where you are now, preventing you from thinking.

Do you know what happens when you stop thinking? Our mind's control panel goes into "autopilot" and you no longer have control of your life. Excessive fear sets in, takes hold and starts to paralyze you when it comes to making decisions and taking action, preventing you from living a life free from the mental slavery that is anxiety.

Your lack of control over navigating your mind is, in reality, a major anxiety trap. That's why the first step towards freedom from this prison is to stop looking outwards, especially in the direction of harmful projections or memories, and stop insisting on answers that don't exist in these two spectra. Then you have to look inside yourself, trying to understand the "why" of each of them. And not the "why".

When you understand why, something happens to you. Regardless of the monster that appears in front of you and makes you want to run away, fighting anxiety is no longer a losing battle. On the contrary, you now have new resources, skills that will take you to higher heights, because, after all, you've gone through the experience and seen that fear and anxiety are just a part of you, and not who you really are.

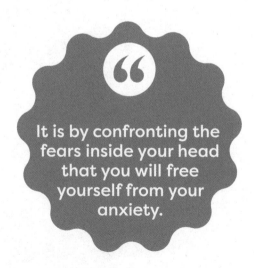

> It is by confronting the fears inside your head that you will free yourself from your anxiety.

The moment an individual confronts each of his fears, he will invariably have one of two reactions: fight or flight. Running away has kept him where he is to this day. So the way forward is to learn that confrontation is liberation, within what he believes to be real in his life. But remember: the struggle takes place inside the mind, because this struggle is internal.

To fight the enemy, you have to dissect it, study it, understanding every detail in order to strengthen yourself in the face of its attacks. For this reason, when people list the biggest fears in their lives, when they name the sensations that manifest in their hearts every time they arise, when they perceive the emotions, the associated situations, how, when and where this fear arises, they discover the trigger that sets anxiety off in their bodies. With this simple fact, each human being begins to have greater clarity about themselves, as well as a more refined state of awareness and perception so that they can then intervene directly at the root of the problem.

Fear lives in people's intellect, with anxiety as its emotional tenant. This is how it takes on a series of negative values, such as displeasure, irritability and anguish in the field of emotions. Being an intellectual construct, anxiety is formed on the basis of your past experiences, related to the memories you have, or according to the "archetypes",[1] the models in their pure and simple essence that permeate your life.

---

1. Archetype is a concept widely explored in philosophy and psychology to demonstrate patterns of behavior experienced by a character or a social role. Basically, the mother, the sage and the hero are examples of archetypes, and all these "characters" have characteristics that are percebidos in a similar way by all human beings. (N.A.)

However, once unbalanced, anxiety is capable of disconnecting human beings from their essence, showing a clear lack of control over emotions and mental faculties.

The perception of what adds to you and what doesn't, the perception that transcends understanding, has long been disconnected due to the imbalance of anxiety. Have you ever seen a dog or cat eat everything they're offered? Even if they're starving, they won't always accept it if their instincts tell them not to. Human beings, on the other hand, even though they are endowed with discernment and are therefore more evolved on the animal scale, are still capable of eating anything they are given or listening to any rubbish they are told to listen to because, unlike animals, who have not disconnected from the intelligence and essence that manifest and drive all of life, people are chronically disconnected.

When we reconnect with this universal intelligence, which some call God, others the Creator Source of the Universe and many other names, life flows naturally and in synchronicity.

> The secret to freedom is not to be ready for anything that happens, but to understand that nothing has power over your heart unless you allow it.

All resistance to liberation is resistance to life. As long as you resist transforming yourself, by changing the way you think and feel, you will continue to be limited and enslaved by the fears that have brought you to this moment.

If you were shocked by this statement, get used to it. You will only stop being a slave to anxiety by transforming your life. Start with your choices, understand how you feed yourself physically, mentally and spiritually, concepts that I will cover in this book.

> The fight against anxiety begins when you decide to face your fears. If you don't have the energy for this confrontation, seek strength by looking at things more simply, as small micro-goals to be achieved. This will strengthen your inner self for even greater achievements.

You need to understand that small victories reconnect your essence to the world of achievement. It is precisely because of the disconnection with their sacred essence that many people are currently stuck in the mere mental and bodily aspects of their lives. Consequently, this disconnection with the source from which life comes is what keeps you simply surviving, and not living in abundance.

Think about it with me: normally, we want to fix the things that come our way; we try to adjust them when we think they're not right. However, the truth is that we have to "fix" ourselves to ensure that everything is fine, whatever happens. You will adjust things according to your internal state. This doesn't mean that you have to conform to the world, but your perception will be so different that it will no longer be able to affect you. Realize how profound this realization is:

"WHEN AN INDIVIDUAL IS TRULY FREE, HE ALLOWS THE OTHER TO BE FREE TOO, EVEN IN ERROR".

The only thing you can do is become love. With that, your life can be an inviting example of transformation for others. But how do we change to transmute ourselves into love? Simply by adjusting our vision.

As soon as you adjust your vision, you realize that, in reality, there is no such thing as a mistake. What exists is a learning curve. We've been indoctrinated into thinking that we're always making mistakes, but that's a big mistake! It turns out that we're just learning, each at our own pace. But unfortunately, some people keep going wrong at the same point.

Ansiedade

My daughter, now a year old, fell an average of sixteen thousand times before she learned to walk at nine months. This shows that human beings learn to throw themselves and avoid falling, they learn to protect themselves from falling, but they don't learn to walk straight away. He throws himself into the move in order to achieve his goal, but in order to avoid falling, to avoid the pain he feels at not achieving what he wants, he learns to throw a leg, learns to throw an arm, and then, falling sixteen thousand times, getting up another sixteen thousand, crying some of the times, he carries on until he learns to walk.

This lust for life doesn't need to be taught. It is innate in free people, and without it there is no life. At some point you unlearned who you were because the world told you that this or that thing you wanted was wrong. Remember this: It's much easier to indoctrinate someone through fear. But now you know where anxieties come from.

As much as you may have stopped believing in your potential, know that you already have everything in essence inside you. However, at some point, for some reason, you locked these answers away so that you would never get hurt again. Your abilities were temporarily inaccessible somewhere inside you. But remember, nothing is lost! My proposal with this reading is that you rescue each of your strengths without the weight of anxiety.

> The focus of this book is not to discuss religion, but we must bear in mind that spirituality is a fundamental part of the human healing process. And whether you believe in it or not, God is merciful in all his forms, and in his infinite mercy he has provided you with everything you need. You just have to wake up to this reality, or dig up what you've buried. It's all there, and always has been. But as long as you insist on looking for what's outside, hoping for a kind of outsourcing of the miracle, you won't be able to realize that we are all already a true miracle.

MOMENT WITH DR. JU [2]

1. At this point, stop reading for a moment and answer the questions below before continuing. At what point did you stop using the abilities that God has given each of us and that keep us going even when we fall?

....

....

....

....

---

2. Some of these questions were extracted and adapted from the DASS-21 Questionnaire (Depression Anxiety Stress Scale 21)

2. At what point did you allow your thoughts to dominate you and thus stop being moved by your spirit? How did you feel at that time?

....

....

....

....

If you think about it, today's world is driven by anxiety. The way our society functions is over-stimulated all the time, with people involved in endless activities, as well as the presence of countless enemies, such as rejection, lack of acceptance, old age and death. Fear, which causes distress and anxiety, has been an official tool of manipulation since the beginning.

However, fear is as limitless as the human spirit, because it is inversely proportional to it. The more activated the spirit, the less fear and, consequently, the less anxiety. The less activated, the less faith and therefore more fear. So it's like a valence in equal proportion, but based on ignorance and non-acceptance of who you are, coupled with misunderstanding about what you came here to be. Note how a seven-headed beast can arise from this realization.

* * *

For more than a century, cinema has been using the great human emotions to fill the audience's eyes. And speaking of fear, there's a famous scene in Harry Potter and the Prisoner of Azkaban that presents a perfect analogy of the "bogeyman". In the movie, the bogeyman is an ethereal monster that takes the form of the greatest fear of each student at the magical school, varying from one individual to the next, sometimes being the evil teacher, sometimes the giant spider, the menacing snake or a dementor. Following this line of reasoning, our bogeymen can take the form of the fear of hell, the loss of a mother or father, the end of a relationship, material scarcity, fear of death, old age, illness or even prosperity.

> Fear is multiform and, based on this aspect, it ends up leading to chronic and accumulated stress in response to the continuous processes of fight or flight. Without a genuine break for the body to restore itself, the stress levels that keep the body functioning start to generate problems in other structures, as well as simply maintaining the stability of its behavior. As a result of this stress dysfunction, the person becomes paranoid, neurotic and defensive.

In reality, the worst thing about fear is that it prevents you from discovering your identity. This is the main way the devil – or whatever you want to call the destructive force of life – works, because it's much easier to stop something extremely powerful in its early stages than during a real avalanche in progress. It's much easier to stop the growth of a life at the beginning than after it becomes aware of who it is. All the devil wants to do is stop spectacular people with very simple and small things, like tying an elephant to a string because he doesn't know how powerful it is, just as was done in circuses.

All people in a constant state of anxiety and depression live governed by past traumas or fear of the future, but the last place they are is in the present..

Bear in mind that the solution to curing anxiety begins with the awakening of acceptance. I've never seen someone, for example, be angry with a reality that is consistent with what they have in their heart. I've never seen someone afraid of what they fully accept in their heart. Therefore, fully accept life from your inner perspective, because everything else we see from the outside is just a mental construction perceived through the "filters" we apply to the world according to our imagination.

Imagination is a mental faculty that allows human beings to dream and visualize. So, within this context, everything we have in us was primarily created in our mind, and everything around us may have been created and manifested by someone else's mind. Imagine it this way: your mind is fertile ground, the problem is that you often don't know where the seeds that are being planted in that ground came from.

MOMENT WITH DR. JU

1. Were the seeds germinating in the fertile soil of your mind planted by you or by other people?

....

....

....

....

2. How were the people who planted those seeds? In a state of fear or in a state of fullness?

....

....

....

....

3. What else could come from this planting?

....

....

....

....

4. Could the fear of those who love you most have contaminated your heart without you realizing it? What has it generated in you?

....

....

....

....

You've probably heard, or even said, the expression "I'm afraid to think". But once you know that running away from your fears makes you stagnate, you have to face the unknown. This is nothing more than the distance between one thought and another. It is in this unexplored terrain that silence manifests itself, where there is an emptiness, just a space, which is usually ignored by most people. Fortunately, there is nothing to fear in these spaces, as you can just observe your thoughts and immerse yourself in the pauses between them in complete silence. This will make you realize the movement of thinking and finally understand that you are not what you think, since thoughts are just states that we experience, and these states change constantly.

The sum of thought and silence manifests your interaction with your existence in life. In other words, you understand that you create the movie of your life and determine when and how it takes place in your head, because you are the author, scriptwriter and director of your thoughts.

How many times have you created a fairy tale or a horror movie in your head? In both cases, you will always be the designer responsible for the movie played in your mind. Anxiety, however, when it presents itself at an inappropriate intensity, causes suffering and functional impairment. A person who has suffered a trauma and has been unable to free themselves from it believes that the trauma defines who they are. But don't forget: your past doesn't define who you are or who others are.

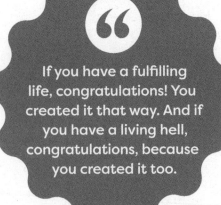

If you have a fulfilling life, congratulations! You created it that way. And if you have a living hell, congratulations, because you created it too.

MOMENT WITH DR. JU

1. What movies and/or stories have you been creating in your mind?

....
....
....
....
....
....

2. How often have they been projected onto your "mental screen"?

....
....
....
....
....
....
....

Until you free yourself in your heart from all the ties you have created, you will still be a slave to the illusions you live.

Before moving on to the next chapter, analyze the first fear presented, the fear of rejection. This step will mark your first steps towards freedom from anxiety.

The fear of rejection runs deep and can be linked to human beings from the time they are born and can manifest itself in any environment.

When you don't feel part of something, rejection takes over your intellect, causing a strong sense of not belonging that generally persists throughout your life and is most often linked from the gestational stage to early childhood.

Based on this, I want you to think of three situations that you carry in your heart in which the feeling of rejection has occurred in a profound way, and then write them down. Then describe a purpose, a really strong reason, that would be able to free you from this feeling.

1

....

....

....

....

....

....

....

2

3

CHAPTER 2

ANXIOUS OR DEPRESSED?

"And he made man in his own image and likeness, to have dominion over all things..."

(Gn 1:26)

"... But first, man must master his own heart."

(Juliano Pimentel)

As we saw at the beginning of this book, anxiety has been a natural human process, since stress has always been present in people's daily lives. A certain amount of anxiety is linked to maintaining life and our productivity. It's normal, therefore, for you to feel sad, distressed and to experience emotional changes from time to time. Suddenly, you may feel a bit apathetic at a certain moment, feeling tired, exhausted or irritable. However, remaining like this all the time is a warning sign.

When a person starts to look at reality as if everything has lost its color, leaving only a black and white world, this is a clear indication that they are losing pleasure and interest in their activities, in other words, nothing gets them excited anymore. By disconnecting from life, we can say that this person has crossed the anxiety threshold and is now suffering from a depressive syndrome – remember that a syndrome is a set of signs and symptoms that show a fixation on certain patterns.

When it comes to such a hot topic, you may be wondering whether anxiety always becomes depression, after all, the symptoms are similar. You see, when anxiety is sustained at a high level, it ends up generating a bodily exhaustion that tends to culminate in depression or burnout – generalized fatigue on the part of the individual, responsible for compromising all their physical, mental and emotional functions. When a person is exhausted to this point, anxiety can trigger depression.

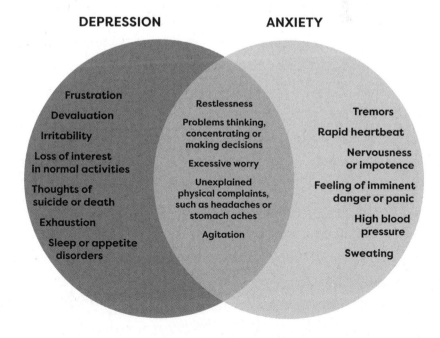

Ansiedade   63

People in a depressive state are not always easily diagnosed, as they present very different pictures. As shown in this diagram, anxiety and depression will always intersect, but the full presentation is different. Both anxious and depressed people can be agitated, both can worry a lot and have difficulty resting, concentrating, thinking or making decisions. Some people may also present with systemic complaints that will most likely not be correctly diagnosed during a routine consultation.

At this point, no matter how much you stop what you're doing, you feel tired. They don't have restful sleep and can't recover. Then comes excessive worry and fear.

Speaking of fear, you've already seen what the fear of rejection can do. But what can the fear of inability do to a person's life?

THE FEAR OF INCAPACITY

The second on the list of seven fears, the fear of incapacity, reminds us of the feeling of weakness, insufficiency and impotence.

People who feel incapable suffer because they have very low self-esteem. They see themselves as disposable and unworthy of receiving love from other people. In this state, they feel they don't have the power to achieve what they want, because they don't recognize their real value. For this reason, when we take a closer look at pathological anxiety and depression, we need to understand that at some point the person has completely lost their strength, and may even believe that they never had the strength to get out of the situation that sank them, and all of this is invariably enhanced by the fear of incapacity.

But remember: it doesn't have to be that way.

The story you're about to read belongs to Karin, one of the first students in the mentoring program I run with a focus on full health. Based on her example, I want to show you how it is possible not to let yourself be defeated by the fear of incapacity and, consequently, to free yourself from the clutches of depression.

I finally discovered that I could be loved

I've battled depression all my life. At the age of 10, when I was on a beach with all my family, I thought: "Why don't I just die?". I still remember seeing my parents and siblings on the beach and the thought suddenly coming to me. "Why don't I die now?". I was only 10 years old, and this thought came back to me from time to time.

I was a child who grew up amid a lot of relationship difficulties, especially with my mother. I was beaten up a lot by her and we fought constantly. I suffered from mood swings that made me wake up feeling good and, five minutes later, hate the world. After another five minutes, I could be humming.

My mother always said that I didn't want to get a husband because I was too volatile, but when I turned 19 I got married, and life seemed to have taken a break during my early 20s. I felt good, and I got married because I wanted sex, and at that time the way to get sex was to get married. Besides, I was already in college and wanted to get out from under my mother's wing.

I was married to my first husband for five years, until he said he wanted to move in with his mother and, as I didn't agree, he left and I stayed. After that, I met my son's father. Felipe was born when I was 26 years old. Soon after I had my son, I started to feel very sleepy, so I slept day and night. He and I slept practically all day. Even after I put him in nursery at 5 months so that I could go back to work, it was a very difficult time, because I still felt so sleepy and very tired. I didn't want anything any more, I didn't want that life any more, I was thinking of giving him to someone else.

Life wasn't going well again. Then, when I turned 35, I moved to the United States and met my second husband, Charlie. I was then in my forties, and thoughts of death began to recur, along with that terrible bad mood and constant sleepiness. Worried about the situation, Charlie encouraged me to seek psychiatric help, even though he himself didn't have much faith in treatment. At the time, I was diagnosed with depression, and from that moment on more than twenty years passed in which I lived on medication. I always started with a certain dosage, until it no longer worked and the dosages were adjusted or the medication replaced.

I carried on like this until December 2017, when I weighed a hundred kilos, was already diabetic and had high cholesterol. I started taking medication for cholesterol and diabetes, and all this made me very afraid of going blind. So I decided to look for something that could help me regain my health, and that's how I found Dr. Juliano's content on YouTube. Everything he said made a lot of sense. Some things I already knew, like the dangers of sugar, but the information about gluten was new to me.

With the courses, the detox and the fasting, I arrived in September 2018 weighing 75 kilos. My diabetes had disappeared, my cholesterol had normalized and I didn't need to take any more medication. But it was in December of that year, during one of Dr. Juliano's events in Orlando, USA, that I had my turning point. The opportunity arose to go on a week-long transformation journey, and I remember going into the event without many expectations, but on the very first two days of class, during a guided meditation, which I thought lasted no more than two minutes, when in fact it lasted 45, I felt loved by my mother and my son. Although I don't remember the meditation itself, there was a process of forgiveness, because I felt light, good and loved.

I never understood how people could love me, but at that moment I felt loved. And after all the re-education I went through, I finally overcame my depression. Before I had this experience, it was as if my head lived in a bucket full of used car oil. After all the changes in my life habits and the meditation, it was as if this oil became clean and then disappeared. For the first time I began to have space in my head, which I hadn't had before. Everything was always very difficult, my thoughts didn't move and I had to force myself to think. But after all the transformation I'd accepted, I felt a huge sense of relief. It really was as if the weight I had lost in my body had also disappeared from my head.

Since 2019 I've been living without any medication for depression, and everything in my life has only improved. I started to think more fluently, to be good-natured and less picky. My husband noticed all the changes in my weight and mood, because I never woke up in that miserable bad mood that made me just want to go to sleep. I woke up feeling light, able to face a cold shower – even at dawn! – and not wanting to bite anyone afterwards!

Karin K., 65, New York, USA.

SLAVES TO MEMORY AND DISTORTED SELF-IMAGE

Depression is not weakness. The fact is that the depressed person starts channeling all their energy in a specific direction that doesn't help them at all. Let's face it, a person with this kind of power over their own life is an incredible human being. I always teach my students that their history doesn't determine who they are, and my role is to show them that their lives are a full possibility that is renewed every day! Karin's freedom began with accepting this new way of thinking.

When human beings are slaves to their memory, they can't get out of their "mental library", so they spend their whole lives inside it. But this "library" is designed for you to access information whenever you want, in order to analyze something you're going to use in the present, not to stay cooped up inside it.

And so we come to another aspect, which is that the depressive doesn't take action. They live inside the lie they've built for themselves, inside a lie of pain, a horror movie, without understanding that they have the full power to build whatever they want in their mentality.

Returning to Karin's story, she finally discovered how to get in and out of her own mental library. In addition, for the first time in her life, she also learned that she was facing a process of changing her self-image and self-esteem due to depression. The process of freeing herself from who she thought she was allowed her to seek the path of losing weight and restoring her health, which consequently led her to see a way out of her mental prison.

> The past does not define who you are, nor who others are!

Self-image can be summed up as how you see yourself, and self-esteem is how you relate to what you see. When a person stops seeing themselves well, there are two possibilities: either they deny themselves or they accept themselves.

Remember? Every acceptance generates liberation! When people don't accept themselves, they end up getting angry, often developing a rage, dissatisfied with what they see on the outside. Even though everyone tells them that they are capable of achieving something, inside they believe that they are not. And then they become inflamed, because the only thing that can really irritate a human being is when they are faced with a reality in the world that confronts their immutable values.

What needs to be made clear is that when a person in a depressed state gets angry, they abandon their position of apathy and raise their energy, even if in a limited way. And this is because, deep down, they know they are capable of incredible feats, even if intellectually this seems so far away.

"Be angry, but do not sin.
Let not the sun go down on your wrath."

(Eph 4:26)

Have you ever wondered why most people suffering from depression know the day and time it started? This reveals human beings who have not been prepared for the struggle and adversity of life. If the person knows exactly when it started, it may not even be depression itself, but rather the experience of a traumatic event that they were unable to overcome. For example, the death of a loved one, a betrayal by a loved one, the loss of a child, financial difficulties. And because her body is sick, intoxicated and weakened by altered hormones, she can't overcome the challenges because she lacks energy. When I say that human beings are weak, I'm not referring specifically to emotional weakness, but to physiological weakness.

> Did you know that Bhutan is one of the happiest countries in the world? Located in the far east of the Himalayas, Bhutan does not have a significant rate of depression. And do you know why? Because the locals have a habit of reflecting on death, rather than ignoring it or treating it as taboo[3]. As a result, the Bhutanese, who are asked to think about death five times a day, see it as part of life. When you understand the finiteness of your life, you value every second.

---

3. Available at: https://www.bbc.com/portuguese/noticias/2015/05/150504_vert_tra_butao_felicidade_ml. Accessed on: May 2022.

GAME CHANGING

How many people are cured of untreatable diseases by themselves? Cases of spontaneous healing are present throughout medicine. When a person decides to live every second uniquely in love, anything is possible. Why is it that so many people are transformed by fatherhood, motherhood, near-death experiences or even a diagnosis or accident?

Simply because every major realization of life and imminent death can be a game changer, i.e. a turning point in a person's life.

If you know when and in what situation you decided to live in the past in order to avoid the pain of a present you don't accept, you have the key to your liberation in your hands!

"

If at this point you are already worried because you identify with one (or more) of the symptoms shown in the figure on p. 63, pay attention and answer the following questions:

MOMENT WITH DR. JU

1. Do the symptoms you've identified paralyze your life? Please comment.

....
....
....
....
....
....
....
....
....
....
....
....

2. How do you deal with these symptoms in your daily life?

....

....

....

....

....

....

....

....

....

....

....

....

IT'S NOT JUST A QUESTION OF THE MIND

When thinking about depressive and anxious states, most people see them only as a matter of the mind. But that's not quite how it works. Both are also related to hormones. So the mind, hormones and various other areas of life undergo changes as a result of anxiety. Cortisol, popularly known as the "stress hormone", melatonin, or the "sleep hormone", and even basal temperature are altered in the face of anxious processes, and the individual needs to organize each of these aspects so that in the end their life is not disrupted as a whole.

Despite these metabolic changes, the good news is that the solution to all of this is much simpler than you might think, because by disarming the fears listed in this book, applying the concepts I'll teach you in each chapter, you'll have everything you need to change whatever you want in your life.

* * *

Finally, remember that anxiety and depression change human perception of events in some ways. One is guided by the imagination, the other by memory. Both navigate the same sea: hormones and the body, which responds as it can to these changes. Chronic anxiety maintained for a long time wears down the body to the point of depression. There are situations in which people don't understand that they are already depressed, while they have always been anxious and depressed because of traumas.

In addition, both anxious and depressed people fail to respond positively to stress. However, as I said at the beginning of this book, stress is part of life, and a person needs to be able to cope with the ups and downs. Otherwise, what will become of them? The answer lies in the very aspects of being, in everything that makes up a human being. In how this being, from his intellect, means everything, faces all things, immerses himself in all situations and in how he interprets them in his innermost being on a daily basis, so that this triggers an effect both physically and emotionally and socially. In every situation in our lives we are invited to expand.

> Imagine a lion loose in the street, far away from you, and notice how you feel. Now imagine it's in front of you. If it's far away, it's still a potential threat, which could generate anxiety and an initial reaction of fear. Now, if the lion is very close, panic may set in, thus triggering the fight or flight process. (Thankfully, most fears don't concern a real lion in front of us!) Such a rush of adrenaline means that we are unable to generate a correct adaptation of feelings, and the secret to this lies in the transcendence achieved purely and simply by breathing.

In the next chapter, you'll discover how to use one of the most powerful tools to gain control of yourself and immediately stop the anxious symptoms attacking your body.

CHAPTER 3

THE EXIT DOOR

> "The Spirit of God made me, and the breath of the Almighty gave me life."
>
> (Job 33:4)

In the previous chapters, you learned more about anxiety, understanding that its origins go back to the beginning of the human species and that its imbalance can cause even greater damage, such as pathological anxiety and major depression.

Once you've understood how it works, it's time to get to know the main tool you can use whenever you're faced with day-to-day anxiety. This tool has been worked on and known for over 8,000 years, and your life began with it. Get to know breathing, the way out of the feeling of imprisonment caused by anxiety.

Anxiety, to a certain extent, is expected, due to expectations about life's events. Added to this is stress, which is triggered by a series of internal and external factors such as demands, an exhausting routine and fears. It's possible that you've already been through this or that you know someone who has experienced situations of great stress, such as the loss of a loved one, a redundancy or any other radical change that has triggered an anxiety crisis. Have you ever stopped to pay attention to how your breathing behaves in these moments? If not, I want you to start noticing your breathing in all these circumstances.

To help you reflect on your breathing, answer the following questionnaire.

MOMENT WITH DR. JU

1. Have you ever noticed that when you're in an anxious state, your breathing changes?

....

....

....

....

2. When you're anxious, are your breaths short or deep?

....

....

....

....

3. When you experience an episode of anxiety, is your breathing slow or fast?

....

....

....

....

4. When you feel anxious, is your breathing light or can it be perceived by those around you?

....

....

....

....

THE BREATH OF LIFE

The world's oldest medicine, Ayurveda, has its origins in India. It essentially uses natural means such as herbs, plants and oils to treat health and sees breathing as a layer of life, in which its own expression manifests. This medicine assumes that people have a level of energy proportional to their consciousness and breathing capacity.

According to Judeo-Christian philosophy, life began with the breath of God. Therefore, life has always been related to breathing, while death has always been associated with exhalation. Inevitably, we all hold the breath as the basic source of acquiring the energy necessary for life, and by mastering this tool you will begin to finally free yourself from the shackles of anxiety.

> Notice that, in everyday life, we're not aware of our breathing, just as we're not aware of our heart beating or how our eyes or ears work. When our organs are working properly, we're not aware of them. Imagine what it would be like if we had to think every day to make each organ work. We wouldn't be able to do anything else in life!

Our body has been prepared to make what it needs work optimally. However, there are situations, such as anxiety, that make your brain believe that your lungs are breathing properly, that you are functioning properly and that this has become your normal, but this is not the case. From a neurological point of view, you've simply accommodated, and that's the term, "accommodation", which consists of a state of remaining in a situation to which you've become accustomed. In the case of breathing, you believe that you are breathing in the best possible way.

Have you ever noticed that, when tired, we have a breathing pattern that involves more movement of the chest? Most anxious and tired people breathe in an apical manner, which consists of breathing predominantly from the chest, while those who are calmer tend to breathe in abdominal and mixed patterns.

To make this clearer, you should know that breathing only occurs through negativity in the lungs, which can be promoted primarily by the diaphragm muscle or by the ribs, with the activation of other muscles.

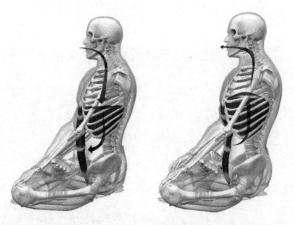

THE PROCESS OF INHALING (LEFT), WHICH LOWERS THE DIAPHRAGM, AND EXHALING (RIGHT), IN WHICH THE AIR COMES OUT, SHOWING THAT THE WHOLE STRUCTURE IS MOBILIZED.

Breathing through the nostrils, with the diaphragm activated, mobilizes all the viscera and fills the lungs from their base. The diaphragm moves and mobilizes the liver, intestines, stomach and heart. This temporarily alters all the body's structures through breathing, puffing up the belly.

* * *

Although we breathe incessantly while we are alive, it is very rare that we are actually present to the act of breathing. However, as already mentioned, this act is a tool capable of altering our entire state when faced with a stressful situation that results in anxiety, eliminating unwanted symptoms as soon as we adopt an appropriate breathing pattern.

The following testimony recounts the process of one of my students discovering and becoming aware of her own breathing, which changed her life forever.

Breathing saved me

I was about to have a heart attack in the corridor at college, and it felt awful. The year was 2019, and for the first time I thought I was going to die, at the age of 21. My left arm started to go numb, and I remembered having heard that when the left arm goes numb, it's a sign of a heart attack. My breathing quickened and my heart was pounding, trying to get out of my chest. My vision was blurred and a crying fit set in.

From an early age, anxiety was all around me. I was a child known for overeating at parties and family gatherings, despite the disapproving looks, which caused me to become even more compulsive, to the point of vomiting everything after eating so much. What's more, I was never able to face it calmly when something new came along. Whenever something unfamiliar came along, something new, I suffered in anticipation. It could be the best thing in the world for me, but I always had enormous anxiety, wondering if I would win something, if something would happen, if I would be successful or not.

It was a constant routine for me to suffer in anticipation of things happening in my life, and this was reflected directly in my body. Sometimes it could be a crying fit. At other times, I seemed to get a tic in my hand, so agitated I was. I'd get migraines, body aches and severe hair loss. I felt knocked down. But I didn't understand that they were anxiety attacks, until the biggest one happened, that day when I thought I was having a heart attack at university.

When that generalized malaise finally passed, the doctors explained to me that it was an anxiety attack because, despite all my bodily reactions, the clinical tests were always within the normal range. Before that episode, I didn't really understand what was happening to me, but as I thought back to other intense events in the past, I realized that they were all related to the same factor, anxiety.

What drove me crazy was trying to control everything that we don't really control, because it's part of life. Study, work and personal life were all targets for my desire to control, and when the Covid-19 pandemic hit in 2020, everything got worse. The crises became recurrent, due to social isolation. I would scream, locked in my room, to see if this feeling would come out of me. After this more intense state had passed, I would ask myself why I had done all this. I felt like the weakest person in the world and I was destroyed.

No matter where I was or what the situation was, everything could change in a matter of seconds. On one occasion, I arrived for a pilates class in a not very good state, because hours earlier I had received a call from my brother saying that our mother was in hospital because she had taken ill at home. Even after calling her and making sure she was all right, my head wasn't in the class, and my helplessness in the face of the series of exercises made me run crying to the gym bathroom, where I was helped. I could barely speak, but when I uttered the word "anxiety" in a broken voice, the teacher took me to a well-ventilated area. I needed air to breathe again.

Today I say that breathing saved me, because I was only freed from this martyrdom the day I finally learned to breathe. It all starts with breathing. My crises were very marked by shortness of breath, so when I finally learned what breathing was, through my first meditation class, life changed forever. The episode at the gym was the last one, because from then on I started to put into practice the breathing exercises I learned in the first immersion I did with Dr. Juliano, during the Travessia, which brought me into contact with my breathing, and this completely relaxed me.

Raphaela Barreto, 23, João Pessoa-PB

FEAR OF ABANDONMENT

In the previous chapters, fears such as rejection and incapacity were presented, and when we talk about breathing patterns, the degree of energy and liveliness is closely correlated to feeling fear. Just as your mental state has power over your breathing, your breathing also has power over your mental state. However, the crux of the matter is that breathing is not about the mind. Breathing is a bridge from the mind to the spirit. By practicing conscious breathing when you find yourself in an anxious state, you not only break your pattern of anxiety, you also create a bridge to the possibility of liberation from suffering. Many students report that during certain breaths in meditative processes, they experience the same symptoms in their bodies as during a panic attack. However, during meditation, the mind's perception of these bodily responses becomes very different and free of fear.

Do you want to see another fear that is unmasked through conscious breathing? The fear of abandonment. The fear of abandonment is a figment of our imagination that we need other people to complete us. However, this happens when we don't have a connection with God, so we really find ourselves alone without others. In this way, we end up needing others and, in parallel with this, we are sociable beings; this is why, at the basis of everything we live and believe in, there is the family, according to the Judeo-Christian context. But even if we live in a family, the fear of abandonment won't be a threat until we understand that our fullness doesn't depend on anyone other than ourselves and our connection with God.

In the story you'll see below, belonging to my student Luzia, the fear of abandonment was evidenced by questions such as: "Was I not a good enough mother?", "Was I not enough and they had to go to another country to get on with their lives?". But notice how, from the key turning point in her breathing pattern, which initiated all the other changes in her mental state, she freed herself from her greatest fear, putting an end to her anxiety.

Ties of abandonment never again

Throughout my life, I've always found everything very complicated. Diabetes, high blood pressure, osteoporosis, uncontrolled thyroid were always conditions that accompanied me, but the worst of all was major depression. I got married, started a family, and when my daughters, who were everything in my life, grew up and got married, they went their separate ways, choosing to live abroad, and that's when the world came crashing down on me.

    I just couldn't accept the fact that they had grown up and needed to look after their own lives. The feeling was that I had lost my reason for living. Soon, the symptoms of deep anxiety and depression began to overwhelm me. Every day became gray, and the thoughts that I had failed as a mother, that I hadn't been good enough and that's why they had abandoned me, were constant. I no longer slept, I didn't leave the house, I ate compulsively, and I felt generalized pain. The despair was so suffocating that on more than one occasion I reached for a firearm in the house, but thank God I took my finger off the trigger at the last moment. My spirituality at that time was almost dead, but today I understand that there was still a thread of hope that kept me alive, and which I clung to when I met Dr. Juliano, through his videos on Youtube, and began to follow his teachings.

    With each step I took in the immersion courses I did with him, I realized that my daughters had not abandoned me, but that I had actually established a relationship of dependence on them by feeding my fear of loneliness. And the meditation practices made me focus on myself, and every depressing thought faded from my mind, making room for full life, gave me awareness of a healthy and abundant life, and a deep connection with God that freed me from the horror of thinking about death to get rid of the pain.

That's how, in the space of a year, I lost around 45 kg, which amazed many people, as I had previously weighed 120 kg. I got rid of binge eating, physical pain and, above all, emotional and spiritual pain. When I finally realized that the abandonment I felt was a mere fantasy in my head, driven by the fear that I had only projected to be bigger than me, the anxiety disappeared, as did the depression. My thoughts stopped being dragged into dark places. With peace re-established, today the bond with my daughters is even greater, free from the weight of attachment and the bonds of the fear of being abandoned, because I live fully with myself, knowing that I am an even better mother for letting my daughters live free and fulfilled on their paths.

Luzia Maria, 59, Goiás.

* * *

When a person puts the center of their life where it really isn't meant to be, waiting for the retribution they would like from someone who can't give it, they will suffer. Luzia, from the moment she learned to change the pattern of her mental state through breathing, completely changed her focus, so as much as her mind tried to direct her thoughts elsewhere, the proper breathing pattern she began to adopt daily was a key element in freeing her mind from the tangle of confusion to which it was stuck.

In my fasting processes, breathing has always been an integral part of all processes of freeing the mind. Most people today are enslaved by the mind, as we've already mentioned.

Now, you might ask yourself:

"How do I stop being a slave to my mind if I have to live off my work to make money?"

"How do I stop being a slave to my mind if I have to do this and that?"

"How do I stop being a slave to my mind if I have an infinite list of things?"

In reality, you'll be a slave as long as you don't realize that you yourself have created this endless list of things, and you're still guided by it.

In this process, breathing is the moment when you completely abstract yourself from all of this and begin to perceive your body and mind without identifying with your thoughts, because all identification generates limitation.

"THE ONLY IDENTIFICATION YOU HAVE TO HAVE IS WITH GOD, WHO CREATED THE ENTIRE UNIVERSE. ANY IDENTIFICATION BELOW GOD IS LIMITING."QUALQUER IDENTIFICAÇÃO ABAIXO DE DEUS É LIMITANTE."

EMBRACE YOUR FEARS

By now, you've probably realized that, in order to live free of anxiety, you first need to understand that, regardless of where you are and what situation you're facing, you need to embrace your fears. Only then will you be able to see that they are not the monster you paint them to be.

"But doctor, how do you embrace your fears?" you might ask. What I can tell you is that it all starts with breathing awareness.

First, you should do the initial exercise presented in this chapter. This will help you to become more aware of your breathing and body and, consequently, have greater control over your breathing.

The moment you begin to exercise this mastery over your body, over your breathing, you will become much more aware. From then on, you will be able to assume that you are aware of your state, and believe "I'm afraid", consciously you are also able to decide that you are only facing a specific situation that causes you fear, but that it is only a temporary obstacle that you are perfectly able to deal with.

Now that you can think about your state, answer the following questions:

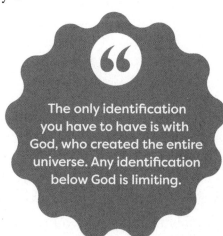

The only identification you have to have is with God, who created the entire universe. Any identification below God is limiting.

MOMENT WITH DR. JU

5. How many times in my life has this situation caused me fear?

....

....

....

....

6. What do I have to do in front of her?

....

....

....

....

7. Am I going to keep running away? Or do I go for it, especially if it's a mental situation?

....

....

....

....

Each of these questions generates a positive confrontation about what you're going through. True confrontation generates liberation, just as transcendence also generates liberation.

I've had students who didn't want to confront their mother, but wanted to transcend. And guess what? Transcendence didn't happen! The path to the much-desired inner renewal only occurs when you completely change your state of being. You transform your entire existence, becoming love, or else you have to resort to confrontation.

When you transform yourself into love, it's easy, but most people can't do that, which is why they need confrontation at a high energy level.

For a better understanding of what high energy means, imagine that you've held back in your heart countless things that needed to be said and haven't been. Remember all the issues that should have been addressed and that still bother you, like heavy burdens that you insist on dragging around with you.

> Siddhartha Gautama said that three things cannot remain hidden for long: the sun, the moon and the truth. Jesus said: "You will know the truth and it will set you free". Commit these two statements to memory, because, however difficult it may be to expose everything that is in your heart, this is the key to true freedom for those you love. Moreover, only in this way will you not be playing roles to please someone else. So never hold back communication and always speak what you need to, putting a hundred times more love into your speech!

In the mind are all the reasons why you didn't speak up or address a subject that you needed to and were put in a certain situation. Everything that is imprinted in our mind carries a high emotional impact associated with it. For this reason, tearing the heart open, exploding and closing it in love is the solution to facing fear in most situations. Exploding lets what has been dammed up in you flow, and closing in love generates what you have always been looking for, which is full connection. At the intellectual level, where the whole thought process takes place, the person promotes a clash in which a series of meanings are generated and, finally, resolves the situation of "vomiting" everything they are carrying in order to relieve their heart.

Although this is a confrontation, it is an act that generates liberation, which is why it doesn't have to be a painful process. By resorting to breathing, your mental state gradually changes.

> **"** During each breath, you will inhale everything you don't have and need, letting go of everything else you used to carry but no longer want in your life. Then breathe in courage, confidence, love, self-esteem and power; and breathe out fear, abandonment, rejection and trauma.

PRANAYAMA

Ayurvedic medicine uses pranayamas to achieve correct breathing, which is capable of healing and preventing serious health problems, as well as purifying and energizing the whole body. In Sanskrit, prāna represents breathing and vital energy, which the Chinese call chi and the Greeks call ruah. Regardless of the language and etymological origin, we will assume all of this as something that gives strength and life to cells and organs. Thus, pranayamas are breathing techniques that help you manage your vital energy, harmonizing body, mind and spirit. That said, imagine now that this breath of life is flowing through your body in some way, starting and ending in different regions. One way to categorize prāna is through vāyus, which means "wind" or "air" in Sanskrit. Check out the list of vāyus below, as well as their locations and respective responsibilities:

VĀYU	LOCATION	RESPONSIBILITY
Prāna	Head, lungs, heart	Movement is inward and downward, and the life force of life. Balanced prāna leads to a balanced and calm mind and emotions.
Apāna	Lower abdomen	Movement is outward and downward, and is related to elimination processes, reproduction and skeletal health (absorption of nutrients). Balanced apāna leads to a healthy digestive and reproductive system.
Udāna	Diaphragm, throat	The movement is upward, related to respiratory functions, speech and brain function. Balanced udāna leads to a healthy respiratory system, clarity of speech, a healthy mind, good memory, creativity, etc.
Samana	Navel	The movement is spiral, concentrated around the navel, like a shaking movement, and is related to digestion at all levels. Balanced samana leads to a healthy metabolism.
Vyana	Originating in the heart, distributed everywhere	The movement is outwards, like the circulatory process. It's related to the cardiac system. Balanced vyāna leads to a healthy heart, balanced circulation and nerves.

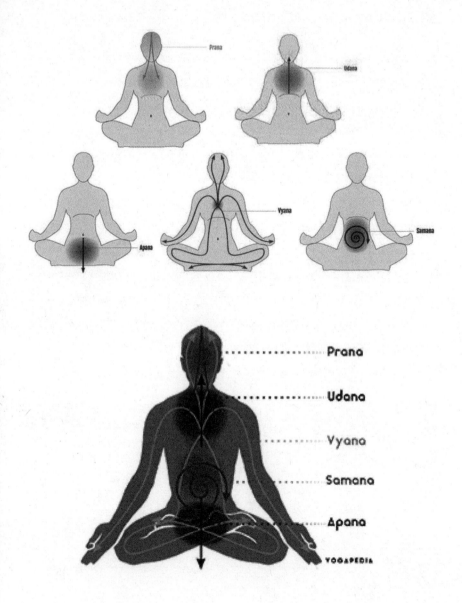

Everyone thinks that breathing is made up of inhaling and exhaling. But what makes inhalation and exhalation exist is what happens between them. Look at it this way: what makes each word powerful is the silence that occurs between them. So the inspiratory pause and the expiratory pause are extremely important if we are to achieve the benefits we want from breathing techniques.

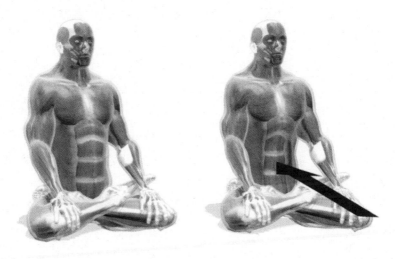

EXHALING AND AGAINST THE ABDOME

BREATHE AND SAY GOODBYE TO DESPAIR

As we saw in my student Raphaela's story, the lack of awareness of breathing can cause such widespread despair that you believe you're having a heart attack. So, to start freeing yourself from the chains you're dragging around, let's start with a very simple and powerful exercise.

First of all, take a half kilo or one kilo bag of rice, beans or any other non-perishable food. Then lie down on the floor and place the bag over your belly, in the navel area. Then breathe slowly for five minutes. With each inhalation – the movement of pulling the air in – the bag should go up, and with each exhalation – the movement of releasing – the bag should go down. This exercise serves to increase your awareness of how the diaphragm works and your mastery of it.

* * *

This chapter has been devoted almost entirely to breathing practice, because if you resort to breathing as taught here, you will have resolved most of the symptoms triggered by anxiety. And speaking of resolving symptoms, in the next chapter we'll look at anxiety and its relationship with immunity. Get ready to breathe like you never thought possible in your life!

MOMENT WITH DR. JU

1. After doing the breathing exercises proposed throughout this chapter, as well as those provided in the QR Codes, record here how you felt.

....

....

....

2. After the registration proposed in the previous exercise, answer the following questions:

a. How long do you want to maintain this state in your life? What is stopping you from having this state in your life?

....

....

....

b. Have you ever felt afraid for no reason? How did this happen and how long did it last? How often does this happen in your life?

....

....

....

c. Have you ever felt like you were going to panic? How did this happen and how long did it last? How often does this happen in your life?

....

....

....

d. Have you ever felt agitated? How did this happen and how long did it last? How often does this happen in your life?

....

....

....

e. Did you have difficulty breathing at any time (e.g. wheezing, shortness of breath without making any physical effort)? How did this happen and how long did it last? How often does this happen in your life?

....

....

....

CHAPTER 4

IMMUNITY THREATENED

> "Be strong and courageous! Do not be dismayed or discouraged, for the Lord, your God, will be with you wherever you go."
>
> (Josh 1:9)

It would be impossible to talk about anxiety without addressing its relationship with the immune system. After all, anxiety is defined by a set of symptoms that attack the body, destabilizing it. Since the primary function of the immune system is to defend us against aggressors, it is essential that you understand how it works.

From now on, you will understand how this system made up of different types of cells, tissues, chemical substances and organs acts on your body and takes care of you, protecting you in particular from the attacks of anxiety.

Imagine a guard dog whose basic function is to guard a territory, preventing enemies from invading it. Generally, this dog doesn't attack those it recognizes as friends. However, if it's too hungry or too agitated, what could end up happening? Yes, that's exactly what you're thinking. It's possible that the animal will attack someone in the house.

This example is to help you understand that your body will always protect you, as long as you provide the necessary conditions for it to do so without hurting itself.

> When we think about the relationship between anxiety and the immune system, the principle is basically this: when there is an internal imbalance in the individual, they can also start to attack themselves and become vulnerable to a series of external factors, such as viruses and bacteria.

To clarify this principle, let's try to get a better understanding of what the human immune system is, a subject that has been covered exhaustively recently. The basic function of this system is to defend the body against invaders. Part of it accompanies us from birth, while another part is acquired, i.e. created through defense cells that react to exposure to a danger (pathogen) that could potentially harm our body, such as the flu or a cold. This division of the immune system is called the innate immune system and the adaptive immune system, respectively.

Defense cells are generally called white blood cells. They are the first line of defense for the most diverse types of tissue in our body. When they detect an enemy, they signal this by releasing chemical substances that attract other cells of the same type to help them.

A general line of defense, such as the Natural Killer cell, for example, has the function of attacking enemies in a more general way. It is the same cell that attacks fungi, viruses and any other invaders. In order to reinforce this attack, the body creates the adaptive immune system, which is a delayed response. After the first stimulus, it takes some time for the body to make use of this defense strategy through antibodies, which serve as signals to take the fight to a more intense level, thus facilitating the functioning of the defense cells and annihilating enemies more generally.

It turns out that the function of this system is to fight microbes, which involves germs, micro-organisms, cancer cells, tissues or organs transported as foreign bodies and anything else that the body doesn't interpret as part of itself, killing them. This complex system is made up of millions of different cells, each acting in a different way to deal with any abnormality. The body reacts daily to attacks from bacteria, viruses, fungi and other types of microbes. So, when we think about the composition of the immune system, there are even organs that act as real defense barriers.

So how does the immune system work in the first instance? Well, we have various so-called lymphoid organs, such as the thymus, as well as lymph nodes, such as the spleen and tonsil.

These organs have immunological functions that vary from place to place. In the intestine, however, we have the presence of something primordial, which is the Peyer's patch, a group of lymphoid cells that is equivalent to 80% of our immune system, all scattered throughout our intestinal tissue.

Okay, but why am I explaining all this? Well, so that you can understand that by using the immune system correctly, feeding your gut properly and removing everything that harms it, you'll be able to silence it when necessary, for example in the case of autoimmune diseases. In this way, it will be able to act as expected, preventing your immune system from behaving like a rabid dog.

We'll go into this in more depth later. Right now, you still need to focus on your breathing.

A "WAR" INSIDE YOU

It's likely that right now there's a "war" going on inside you, because, in addition to constant exposure to dangerous agents such as viruses and bacteria that thirst to invade your body through poor diet and many other unhealthy habits, there's another point that goes beyond the gut.

The entire immune system is governed not only by the intestine, but also by hormones and the vascular system. As well as neglecting our diet and being overly stressed, which leads to an imbalance in the gut and hormones, most people don't do any physical activity and are used to taking hot baths, which does nothing to help maintain the vascular system.

Nowadays, most people are afraid to bathe at room temperature. Cold water trains our capillaries, the thin part of the body's blood circulation. Deprived of this training, the vascular system no longer receives a great deal of help so that it can be mobilized correctly. All these factors add up to a major problem.

In the previous chapter, you were introduced to breathing. When done correctly, it completely alters the return of blood to the heart and, with it, how much blood it throws out every minute, which prevents episodes of tachycardia, high blood pressure and other symptoms responsible for the general malaise caused by anxiety.

Breathing is capable of providing extraordinary benefits for your health, and can be done consciously even when you're taking a simple shower. Speaking of which, have you ever wondered how we got to the point of being afraid of bathing in cold or even room temperature water? One thing I never thought I'd see is people taking hot showers or even "pelando", as they say in Espírito Santo, even in extremely hot regions. The fact is that human beings have settled for the comfort of a hot bath and this has caused some damage to their immune systems.

You see, so far I've only referred to room temperature bathing, I haven't even gotten into the truth of cold bathing, which also has incredible benefits, but for that you need to live in states of very low temperatures.

When our body is exposed to a temperature different from that of the environment, its reaction is to automatically adjust our breathing, because through it we can generate and dissipate heat. If it's too cold, the body will involuntarily start to shake its muscles, so that the movement of the muscle fibers generates heat due to the friction between the cells. As well as putting you into a breathing pattern, this generates vasoconstriction, which is a reduction in the diameter of blood vessels. When we adapt to extreme cold, a kind of "gymnastics" takes place, both in the capillaries and in the peripheral vessels, thus increasing the tolerability of the immune system.

This increase in tolerability happens by training the autonomic nervous system, which is directly related to the immune system and responsible for regulating the functioning of organs that, in theory, we don't control. However, the environment and the way we expose ourselves to it and connect with the cold, nature and breathing can activate or deactivate this immune system.

It is for this reason that states of stress and fear release hormones such as corticoids and adrenaline, which, if left activated for too long, generate negative changes in countless metabolic pathways, including sex hormones, weakening the immune system by keeping the individual in a constant state of alert, in a fight and flight response.

Now you know why anxiety lowers immunity. Simply because it keeps cortisol levels high in the body. Cortisol is the hormone responsible for controlling stress, and it lowers immunity if it is unregulated; however, in the right dose, it is essential for life. Cortisol only poses a risk when it is at excessively high levels for a long time, as this creates problems by suppressing the body's natural defense functions.

But how does cortisol become elevated? To understand this process, we need to remember the fight and flight reaction, the one that was so important to our ancestors. The first thing that happens in a fight or flight situation is the rise in cortisol and adrenaline, and this hormonal response causes your body to have positive or negative results, depending on how it performs.

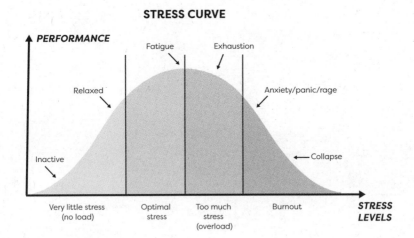

EMOTIONS AND YOUR ANXIETY

An emotion is something short-lived, lasting an average of four seconds and over which you have no control or power. For this reason, it is one of the main factors affecting your level of cortisol, the stress hormone. Associated with feeling, which is how you relate to a given situation, and thinking, which is involved in that situation, emotion can be a determining factor in any anxious state.

Think of emotions in the following way: they are acute reactions triggered by significant internal stimuli (such as a thought or a memory) or external stimuli (a situation or an encounter), intense and short-lived, commonly accompanied by events that are reflected in the body, such as sweating, tachycardia and a cold stomach. Emotions reduce immediate clarity, intensifying the individual's physical sensations. They are common in our species and are enhanced by each person's moral and cultural context.

Primary emotions have three classifications: shock emotion, choleric emotion and affectionate emotion. When processed, a strong meaning permeates this symbology. At this point, feelings emerge, characterized by less intensity and reactivity and greater stability than emotions. This is a major turning point.

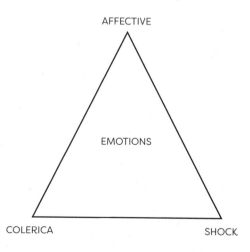

If you live in a constant state of anxiety, how do you feel? Remember: anxiety has a continuous trigger, which causes an increase in cortisol and makes you feel worse and worse. That's why you need to pay attention to your emotions, especially your affect, which is the junction between emotion and feeling. By paying attention to the way you relate to your environment, to the people around you and how this influences your essence or not, you will be acting to strengthen affection, which is a fundamental process for keeping your immunity away from the threat of anxiety.

Your uncontrolled levels of stress, anxiety, panic and anger are mainly responsible for the fall in your defense cycle, which is related to alertness, which in turn is controlled by cortisol, as we have seen.

To illustrate, imagine that you are a barrel with a hole in the middle, one of those wooden barrels with metal rings around it. The hole in the middle never allows the barrel to be completely filled to the top. A person's biological reserve is enough for them to reach the top, but in order for that to happen, they need to plug this hole, or any others they may have. Holes, in this case, are chronic stress, lack of minerals, low hydration and, of course, inadequate breathing. So, as long as you don't have everything you need for your health, your biological reserve capacity will be reduced, as will your body's ability to respond favorably to anxiety.

If you feel like a barrel full of holes, don't be discouraged, because there is always a solution and, best of all, it comes with you. The story I'm going to share below illustrates exactly that and further reinforces the importance of a strategic tool for regaining your breathing and the subsequent control of your health.

I jumped from fear to freedom

As a skydiver, I'm someone who can jump out of an airplane, but until recently I wasn't able to tell myself that I could eat simple broccoli. Ever since I knew myself, I had never been able to eat a fruit or vegetable. I had an aversion to any kind of healthy food, because I couldn't even smell or taste anything that was more natural; it was unthinkable to eat an onion or even an apple, for example.

Until one day I decided to seek help to change and start feeling healthier. After all, one of the biggest problems I was facing was the "accordion effect". I suffered a lot from this, because I took all my emotions out on food. Perhaps it was because I lived far away in another country, didn't have my family around and no one to talk to, that I resorted to the fridge. I even had episodes of putting on fifteen to twenty kilos and then losing the same amount. That was the biggest problem I faced, taking refuge in food in an attempt to get rid of my anxiety.

I reached the point of really seeking liberation. It wasn't even a question of losing weight, because what I really wanted was to break with my mind and finally get out of the prison that anxiety had put me in, not to mention my health, which had been feeling the effects of the bad eating habits I'd always had. It was at this time that I faced the cold bath for the first time – and live! –during a live event promoted by Dr. Juliano, even though I was living in Toronto, Canada, in a different time zone and facing a -25°C winter.

I started taking cold showers every day and, surprisingly, I began to understand that I was able to control my anxiety with this attitude. I was able to understand that my body reacted according to what I put into it, and I realized how it lacked the nutrients that would help my emotional state.

During this process of turning the key through a simple cold shower, I acquired a new vision and self-knowledge, finally being able to recognize that it was up to me to fuel my body so that it reacted positively, not negatively. My life before was based on impulse, because when we cling to it and give in for a moment, we want to eat to satisfy an emotion, and not the real hunger for a need in the body. Every time I fell into this trap, I entered a cycle of failure, telling myself that I had eaten what I shouldn't have because I was a failure.

Today, after finally freeing myself from this whole cycle and facing up to the situation I was in, I really realized that I was stuck like an elephant tied to a stump. But from the mental unlocking provided by the cold baths and the teachings shared in the 7-Day Detox Challenge – a program created by Dr. Juliano to cleanse and activate the body, mind and spirit – I was able to understand that the one who really has the power is me, the one who has the power to say yes or no is me. I can't let my momentary anxiety dominate something that is much bigger.

Priscila Roveri, 36, Toronto, Canada.

THE SECRET OF THE COLD BATH

Priscila's story illustrates how it is possible to protect your body's immunity against the deterioration caused by anxiety. Your brain wants comfort, but you tell it that it needs to go under the cold water. Then your brain learns to obey. It exists to serve you, not to captain your life.

When the body begins to experience peripheral vasoconstriction as a result of the cold, it begins to shiver. In order to produce heat, it shivers, and breathing becomes faster and shorter. That's when you become aware and take long, deep breaths. With this, you realize that your body's sensation changes completely, because the cold is no longer so cold, and you are able, because of the discomfort of the present, to define how you are going to behave, without getting stuck in the past or the future.

This is how the cold bath promotes a state of presence associated with one of the greatest tools you have at your disposal, which is breathing. This activates the immune system, increases the exercise of the capillaries, which are not normally worked on in everyday life, making you train the autonomic nervous system voluntarily and, consequently, get out of the loop of illusions that afflict you.

All of this may not seem like much to some people, but Priscila's mastery of her behavior, thoughts and emotions through the practice of the cold bath allowed her to break away from the stories she had told herself since childhood, which had contributed to her rejecting healthy food until adulthood.

Following on from our list of the seven main fears that trigger anxiety, the fear most closely linked to taking a cold bath is the fear of illness.

In almost everything we do in life, we have to confront certain fears. But even though it may seem daunting, when we face them, however small they may be, we become capable of defeating the bigger ones too. It's the same with fasting. People are afraid to fast because they don't want to die of weakness. By confronting the fear of fasting, you free yourself from other fears.

What's your fear about taking a cold bath? I bet it's getting sick, right? Or fear of the cold...

> When you confront your small fears, the big ones fall away. And you realize that they were only big in your mind..

THE FEAR OF ILLNESS

The fear of illness is among the greatest of the seven, after all, it relates to the fragility and finiteness of life. However, there wasn't always an electric shower, and yet our ancestors survived cold baths very well.

"But, doctor, I can't take a cold bath because of my throat! Imagine a cold bath!"

"But doctor, it's very cold, what if I get sick?"

"I have an earache, doctor, it'll get worse if I take a cold shower!"

Honestly, I've lost count of how many times I've heard objections to cold showers. But what they all amount to is just a fantasy that people create about a simple practice in life.

The cold bath not only provides better vascular quality, but also respiratory quality, which, as I have insisted in this book, is the key to removing the individual from a growing anxiety loop.

Cold bath without fear

In the previous chapter, we presented a series of breathing exercises. When you start the abdominal breathing exercises, you will only do them for five minutes, so observe how you feel after this exercise.

If this is the case for you, we'll break your anxious mental pattern by associating this breathing with relaxing music, so as to keep it constant. This will increase the impact of the exercise.

Get under the shower, turn on the cold shower and do your breathing in a cold bath.

"But what about the story that taking a cold shower causes colds and flu?"

That's a myth. The whole of humanity wouldn't have made it this far if it hadn't been for baths, and those baths were cold! There wasn't always an electric shower, nor was there always an iPhone, a fridge and virtual assistants. So at some point in your ancestors' lives there had to be a cold bath. They had this habit, and it didn't kill them. I've been giving my daughter cold showers since she was born. I mean it. I fell into the icy pool with her as a baby, when she was three months old, and she loved it. She'd come out as hard as a popsicle, but she'd be so happy! She's never had the flu.

> With the practice of the cold bath, you will break a pattern and begin to indoctrinate the body, because the body is the slave of the spirit, just as the mind is the slave of the spirit. But at first, you have to bring the body to be the slave of the mind. At this stage, the person can't even understand that the spirit rules the body and the soul. So you have to understand that the body has become a slave to the mind, and when you say "I'm going to take a cold bath", your body, because of the sensations it has, has to obey your command.

Ansiedade

"IF YOU CAN'T EVEN DETERMINE YOUR BATH, HOW MANY SITUATIONS IN YOUR LIFE CAN YOU NOT DETERMINE?"

If you can't determine that you're stronger than a simple sweet, after all, you keep saying that the sweet is stronger than you, so you can't stop eating it, what great obstacle are you ready to overcome in your life? If the bath is stronger, what will you overcome in your life?

How can you break a circle of anxiety while remaining apathetic?

I want you, the reader, to record your experience, post it and tag me (@drjulianopimentel) in your social media stories. If you get angry with me, feel free to swear at me, that's fine. Now, if you're already anticipating the reaction you'll have when you face the cold shower, pay close attention:

"WHEN YOU'RE IN AN IMMERSIVE PROCESS, MANIFEST THE TRANSFORMATION IN YOUR ACTIONS, SIMPLY DO WHAT NEEDS TO BE DONE."

When you get into the cold bath, keep your breathing slow and deep. You'll notice that when your body comes into contact with the cold water, it will want to take short breaths, just like in an anxiety attack. But your body will behave according to what you want, not how it wants, because the body is at your disposal, not you at its disposal.

Breathing can be practiced at any time in your life. If you're at work, go to the bathroom and apply the techniques you've learned. Five minutes will be enough for you to start enjoying the benefits.

And how do you do that? Basically breathe, focusing your energy on your heart, imagining that the air is entering your lungs and spreading throughout your body. This air calms you, reassures you. Feel the movement it makes when you inhale, its temperature, how it dissipates. All this will happen kinesthetically.

Once you've mastered your fear of the cold bath, you'll be ever closer to overcoming your fear of illness. By the way, in the next chapter we'll get to one of the most controversial topics in the book, which is the effectiveness of anxiety medication.

Before moving on to the next chapter, it is essential that you carry out the following exercise in order to overcome your fear of illness.

There are people who believe a lot of things about diseases. There are people who say that they will live a healthy life because they don't want to get cancer, that everything they do is to avoid getting cancer, but in the end they end up getting cancer.

This is very serious, which is why you need to be clear about your relationship with the fear of illness.

Based on this, reflect and answer:

MOMENT WITH DR. JU

1. Are you afraid of illness? If yes, which one or ones?

....

....

....

2. How do you feel about it? Would it be death? Fear of leaving someone behind? Fear of becoming disabled?

....

....

....

3. How did you deal with this fear before reading this book?

....

....

....

After answering these questions, plan to take your cold shower. During the experience, think: "Am I in the past, the present or the future?". Also, imagine your fear of illness and the relationship you have with it being washed away and down the drain. Can you think about that? Or will it simply be inside your bath in your moment of presence?

Here are some recommendations for you to adopt the practice of taking a cold shower into your routine.

1. For the first three days, start by taking a cold bath for 30 seconds to a minute, then move on to a warm one.
2. From the fourth to the sixth day, take one to two minutes, then turn the water down to lukewarm temperature.
3. In the second week, extend the duration of the cold bath from two to four minutes.
4. In the third week, only take a cold shower for the entire duration of your shower.

Important: Always be aware of your limits and monitor your heart during the activity, and if you're in a very cold environment with sub-zero temperatures, try drinking a hot tea to help your body recover more comfortably.

CHAPTER 5

MEDICINES: ANXIETY CURE OR ILLUSION?

Anxiety. Do medicines cure anxiety? Do they trigger even more anxious symptoms when taken? Does the medicine awaken a greater illusion in the person?

The evil of the century is not obesity, although research shows that it has become an epidemic in the world. Obesity has been around for a long time, but anxiety remains the greatest evil of the 21st century and is present on a large scale, trapping more and more people in a loop in search of a cure through medication.

I bet you know someone who takes medication for anxiety. I'd even venture to say that you yourself have taken, or at least thought about taking, some anxiety medication at some point in your life, perhaps right now. And why am I saying this? Because most people today, when they have some level of anxiety, are looking for a degree of survival, because they are losing peace, losing nights of sleep, losing libido, losing the body they wanted.

Which anxiety medication have you heard of? Perhaps Fluoxetine. Sertraline. Rivotril. Remilev. Clonazepam. Venlafaxine. Reconter. Alprazolam. Bupropion. Escitalopram. Quetiapine. Nortriptyline. Olanzapine. Mirtazapine. Pregabalin. The list is endless...

Now let me ask you a few more questions:

Has the medicine cured your anxiety?

Has the remedy cured any of your acquaintances?

The answer is probably no, and your anxiety is still with you.

Let's say that when you started taking medication to combat anxiety, you imagined that you would be fine, that you would return to normal and that, above all, you would control the symptoms that afflicted you. However, anxiety drugs don't cure. They don't cure people of their problems.

> The remedy is one strategy among hundreds. It's easier to look for the solution in the remedy, but often the easy solution isn't long-lasting, let alone deep enough to generate results.

Pay attention! When we talk about "control", the process is not curative, because in reality you start taking the medicine in order to control one of your mental faculties. Mental faculties were not made to be controlled; they were made to be worked on to the full, to mastery. Whenever you try to control one of your mental faculties, you will end up failing. Save this information and invite all your anxious, compulsive and depressed friends to read this book, because they will all connect in some way with what I'm sharing here.

Look, I'm not saying it's wrong to take medication – even though it doesn't cure anxiety. They are one strategy among hundreds of others. It's easier to look for the solution in the medicine, but often the easy solution isn't long-lasting, let alone deep enough to generate results. In other words, within your mental modus operandi, you end up looking for quick fixes without considering the high price you might pay for it.

The question is: how long will you pay? How long will you hesitate? And when will you take action? I've helped hundreds of thousands of people around the world to get out of their anxiety attacks, to get out of anxious situations in many ways. But to be successful, you have to want it from the bottom of your soul.

This chapter deals with an often neglected topic, which is the impact of anti-anxiety medication on health. The purpose here is to make you aware of the correct use of medication, which should be seen as a bridge to an environment you want to reach, becoming aware of what needs to be done without placing your full expectation and complete faith in a mere pill.

It's true that medication is necessary at times. But the drugs industry, in the context of mental health, is very precarious and old, because, in theory, it only acts on certain areas of the brain. Today, the first reaction people have when they go to the psychiatrist's office is to look for an immediate solution, because they want to get rid of their pain, not only emotionally and psychologically, but also physically, which is often limiting.

However, it's common to come across doctors who have been trained in a Cartesian way and who already have a basis in medication. On some occasions, they even recommend complementing this with psychotherapy, but not infrequently they limit themselves to simply prescribing medication, which is a questionable alternative, as they are only trying to solve a problem by dealing with the symptoms it triggers.

IN SEARCH OF RELIEF

People in pain are in a hurry. That's why when people talk about anxiety medication, they focus on managing the patient's symptoms, not on curing the anxiety itself.

The point is that no one is really cured of anxiety. In fact, in many cases, the person doesn't even know why they are taking the medication, and only has a false impression of improvement, despite feeling that the anxiety remains the same. In fact, the medication manages to relieve the symptoms of anxiety, which allows the person to carry out the therapeutic process through which they will begin the journey of encounter with themselves, their self-discovery and self-knowledge, and in which traumas that gave rise to their pathological anxiety can be released, unblocked and finally extracted.

Until recently, anxiolytic drugs had a series of side effects. The individual gained weight, had their blood glucose and cholesterol levels affected and could trigger hypertension, and the therapeutic effects were very superficial. With this class of medication, the person didn't feel sad, but they didn't stay awake either. They didn't feel anxious, but they couldn't think.

Furthermore, even today in Brazil, most drugs that act on the neurobiochemical axis, which refers to the chemical processes involved in the nervous system, are prescribed by clinical doctors, not psychiatrists. Often, when a psychiatrist comes in, he brings a different approach, but this depends on his knowledge of the interactions between the drugs and what he wants. Some opt for tricyclics, others for serotonin reuptake. However, there are patients who spend decades treating themselves in this way and still claim never to have gotten rid of their anxiety.

Why does this happen? Because the person simply keeps expecting the drug to give them a different response, even after years. When an individual turns to a tricyclic such as triptiline, which has a lower cost, what does their doctor expect to happen? What is the desired outcome in that person's life? If you thought of a reduction in sadness and irritability, you were right. It is also expected to reduce symptoms such as anticipatory suffering, excessive worry, feelings of fear, especially when manifested as adrenaline discharges, associated with increased pressure, heart rate, causing palpitation, shortness of breath, numbness in the hands, lips and cold sweats on the extremities of the body.

In short, all drugs are prescribed with the aim of improving the individual's functions, which is why they act on the reuptake of neurotransmitters so that the brain's internal communication can function as expected again.

The question is: why do failures in brain communication start to occur to the point of triggering anxiety attacks? The answer lies in the mental faculties themselves. As I often say, today's human beings are notoriously slaves to two mental faculties: memory of the past, which can lead to depression when misguided, and imagination, which also, when misguided and fed by traumas, ends up turning into anxiety in all its different degrees, which medicine is beginning to categorize and dichotomize, even though their essence is the same.

> " The core of anxiety comes from two misguided mental faculties: memory of the past and imagination.

TENSION IN THE NERVOUS SYSTEM

To understand how the drug works in the nervous system, let's briefly explore its anatomy. Basically, there is a distance maintained between neurons and in this space, called the synaptic cleft, chemical substances produced naturally by the body are released. However, when there is an imbalance caused by a series of internal and external factors, the drug plays the role of re-establishing neurobiochemical functioning, inhibiting the reception of substances that are damaging the nervous system and thus ensuring that communication between neurons continues to take place and electrical stimulation continues to permeate everyone.

When we think about the relationship between anxiety and neurotransmitters, by keeping serotonin in the synaptic cleft for longer and a certain amount of adrenaline through the action of some drugs, people on medication are usually trying to give vent to the same drives they had in another context of life. They stop expressing anxiety and begin to vent the drive of this faculty, which is imagination, in other contexts, which become other problems in the long term, if this isn't dealt with at its core, at the origin of what caused the anxiety.

However, like everything else in life, something simple can have disastrous consequences. A simple selective serotonin reuptake inhibitor can cause many problems. Medications almost always have side effects, which can include impotence, lack of libido, obesity and, above all, emotional apathy, which means feeling neither joy nor sadness.

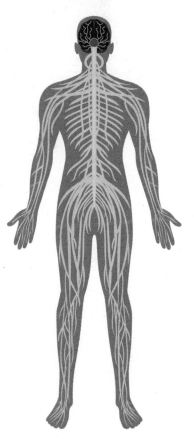

SISTEMA NERVOSO

Even obesity can be seen as a side-effect of this apathy, because as the person is unable to feel any emotion, becoming "robotic", it is possible that they start to relate to food as a way of obtaining some immediate pleasure. This ends up generating a trigger for binge eating, even though the person is treating themselves to fight the compulsion caused by anxiety. There is then a behavioral duality, and the person looks for subterfuges to feel alive.

In certain cases, the complexity goes beyond the neurobiochemical part. Individuals with severe anxiety symptoms need a "brake", a slowdown in their functioning, so that their physiological levels can be adjusted before they enter the behavioral field. Depending on the severity of the individual's condition, they may refuse treatment and may go into a psychotic break or a state of mania, which is often triggered by an uncontrolled anxious state and depends on medication to be regulated.

WHERE DOES THIS FEELING COME FROM?

Imagine the following situation: everything is fine at home, with your husband or wife, with your children, and yet all you feel is sadness. You can't be happy. It can also be a constant feeling of fear, even if you're in the safety and tranquillity of your own home, and be as intense as if you were at gunpoint. This is called persecution mania, a notorious anxiety behavior.

As we have seen, anxiety is present in human history in the form of an instinct that helped us to anticipate danger so that we could protect ourselves. It is therefore natural to be able to deal with physiological anxiety, which also generates a level of metabolic optimization, a level of functional optimization so that we can move, work and defend our family. Now, when it stops being functional and becomes dysfunctional, we have a problem.

DON'T LET "AH, BUT" DOMINATE YOUR LIFE

According to psychiatric specialists, depression has a chance of recovery and cure ranging from 93 to 95%, meaning that a person can take medication, undergo treatment and psychotherapy for a period and never need it again or have depression or pathological anxiety.

It's great to see a psychiatrist say this, because around 99% of people who say they are anxious or depressed actually manage to free themselves from this bondage. I used to ask my students when their symptoms had started, and in a universe of 100,000 people who claimed to suffer from one or both of them, with the exception of one person, who said he had seen life in black and white since the age of 9, everyone else knew the month, day, time and environment in which life turned off.

Humanity is fragile, infantilized, weakened, in need of help more than ever due to countless aspects. That's why we health professionals are here, and that's fine. But people need to understand that they are not victims and that they have responsibility for everything they experience, which is why it is so important to have clarity, discernment and the expression of power to get out of bad situations.

> The anxious person feels that everything is horrible because of their past, so they look to the future and think: "This is going to happen again! I'm going to suffer again". When there is an interpretation of reality that turns to the past, the person ends up moving towards a depressive state; and by looking at the future in a negative way, the path to anxiety is open.

Although depression and anxiety have a high recovery and cure rate, less than half of people are treated. This is because they are tied to events, to suffering. Deep down, they don't allow themselves to stop suffering, and they don't even realize it. If a person discovers that their anxiety disorder was triggered by abuse suffered in childhood, for example, during the therapeutic process they will have to look at this episode from the past and let it stay there. However, it is very common for them to resist this acceptance, reliving those harmful feelings caused by the traumatic event.

> **Every acceptance generates liberation!**

There's no point in insisting on that litany of "Oh, let's go back to the past, let's reframe the screwdriver". Pay attention: when it comes to the past, every acceptance made with maturity and love sets you free. "Ah, but it wasn't fair"; "Ah, but you can't". Don't let this "Ah, but..." rule your life, this justification is no use.

When a person comes into contact with the possibility of a treatment that will enable them to stop suffering, they often turn away because they feel condemned to suffer. As a result, they don't seek out the necessary resources, limiting themselves to the use of medication. It's obvious that this person will spend their whole life undergoing treatment, only to tell their doctor that they haven't improved. It's been proven: medication alone doesn't solve the problem.

THE OUROBOROS OF THE ANXIOUS

At this very moment, thousands of people are trying to understand their own hearts better, because they live in confusion. Sometimes they manifest some kind of illness, or even somatize others. Many remain in toxic relationships.

When we look at people's states of compulsion, without any perception of free consciousness, we can say that they live in the ouroboros dynamic.

The ouroboros is a mythological symbol that depicts infinity and is represented by the figure of a snake biting its own tail. And why does it do this? Because it's not aware of what it's doing. It can only stop biting its tail - which it does because of its insatiable and infinite hunger - when it finally transcends the plane on which it lives. Otherwise, it goes to a new plane and starts biting its own tail within this new stage.

This illustrates the urge to stay in that place in a desperate attempt to feel alive. This is followed by compulsions for food, alcohol, drugs, sex, gambling, shopping, etc. The individual looks to their object of compulsion as a way of filling their existential emptiness, something that is lacking in the depths of their being. For a moment, this emptiness is filled, but then it resurfaces.

They don't realize that they could have come out of their suffering much sooner if they hadn't been so resistant to the new. What's more, their attachment to what they think they know keeps them going. But just as unhealthy thinking led them towards illness, a thought of faith creates an architecture capable of getting them out of that environment, no matter how intellectualized they may be. This new thought transmits security and transcends the intellect.

As we'll see below, a positive and sufficiently strong belief in something Supreme - which I'll call God here - is capable of imploding unhealthy thinking and dragging the human being upwards.

HERO OR VILLAIN?

When we think more deeply about the issue of anxiety medication, Brazil is currently the champion in the use of anxiolytics[4]. The problem is that many of them are used unnecessarily.

Some people attribute their own salvation from anxiety to a medication, while for others it can represent their downfall. But, after all, is this really the responsibility of the medication itself? Obviously not. Medication is nothing more than a tool and, as such, it can be used to save lives as well as destroy them, if administered incorrectly.

As we reflected at the beginning of this book, it's up to you to project a fairy tale or a horror movie in your mind. You can be either the hero or the villain in your relationship with anxiolytics, depending on how you use it.

Millions of lives have been saved by antibiotics and other medications, but there are appropriate times to use these drugs. There is, however, a certain disregard for alternative treatments, which are not drugs, which have no meta-analysis, double-blind randomization, and this is a very serious problem.

---

4. According to recent data from the World Health Organization (WHO), Brazil has become the most anxious country in the world. Available at: https://exame.com/ciencia/brasil-e-o-pais-mais-ansioso-do-mundo-segundo-a-oms/. Accessed on: Apr. 2022. (N.E.)

Every year, clinical practices receive a flood of patients reporting that they have tried everything and nothing has worked, things that have not been validated, tested and matched in articles. This doesn't mean that they don't work, but often that patients have mistakenly consulted untrained people.

How many times have you heard of someone who has undergone "rabbit's foot" therapy - or whatever it's called - and it hasn't worked, and that the person has spent worlds and funds on it, and has tried everything, but is still totally decompensated, without resolving their anxiety attacks? There are brilliant people who spend most of their lives enslaved by anxiety, because of traumas they've suffered. You may be like that too, you may have some hang-ups and live with them for many years. But now pay attention: when you realize that it is in the confrontation in love that complete liberation occurs and that when you simply bring a fact of clarity from unconsciousness to consciousness, your locks will dissipate completely.

For there to be a substantial transformation, you have to face up to the misery in your life, because this is when the desire is generated, the will to turn the tables and give up suffering. In this process of facing your own life, you can't see your misery as a burden. Rather, it is an awakening that invites you to the mercy of life in its fullness, of universal intelligence, of Jesus Christ, of God, of whatever you want in your life to manifest a new level of existence that you have never dreamed of.

Thousands of people have come to me for health, energy and weight loss. However, the basis of all this does not lie in losing fat. Losing weight is easy, but getting to the root cause of obesity by recognizing your own misery and finding out which part of your life you don't want to face, which is why you stay sick, is another matter.

"

I fully believe that it's possible for human beings to heal themselves and the illusions they create, because that's the whole point: they have to heal themselves from what they've created against their own lives.

"

Finally, I'd like to reiterate that each person has a completely different degree of complexity and social impact on the family, which is why the use of medication to combat anxiety cannot be analyzed in a simplistic way. Especially when it comes to severe anxiety, drug treatment is necessary. However, as we have seen in this chapter, medication alone does not solve the problem. Medication is intended to reduce symptoms, and the pharmaceutical industry has gone to great lengths to improve drugs, but it won't create a miracle in your life. You have to do your part.

If you really want to free yourself from the slavery of anxiety, you first need to want to get out of where you are. The process of transforming yourself has to be a conscious act, because your life is already full of compulsion, your obesity or excess weight is enough, your addictions are enough. After all, the pains you carry are dictating your life today - or the catastrophes you collect.

Based on this, reflect on the following questions, and then answer them:

MOMENT WITH DR. JU

1. How long do I want that for my life?

....

....

....

....

2. How long am I going to maintain this level of suffering, pain and relationship that I have with my pain and suffering?

....

....

....

....

3. What should be my next step towards a life free from the traumas of the past?

....

....

....

....

CHAPTER 6

THE MICROBIOTA AND ANXIETY

By now, you've seen how and why anxiety has taken control of your life. We've presented anxiety from its origins as a natural phenomenon for human survival to its becoming one of the most dangerous diseases in the contemporary world. But now that you've learned that breathing is a powerful weapon to unlock you from the most exacerbated symptoms of anxiety, in this chapter we're going to go one step further, this time learning how to free ourselves from the yoke of anxiety through food.

In the chapter on immunity, it was said that there was a "war" going on inside you. This war not only refers to the battles between your defense mechanisms against harmful agents, but also to your own inner ecosystem, or rather, your intestinal microbiota. The microbiota, or intestinal flora, is made up of trillions of microorganisms that inhabit the intestine and are responsible for maintaining the vital functioning of the body. They are essentially bacteria and, before you turn up your nose, know that our bodies contain two types of bacteria, good and bad.

Beneficial bacteria are responsible for receiving everything that reaches the intestine and extracting the nutrients needed to keep us alive and healthy, redistributing this nutritional load to the bloodstream, brain, bones and other components of the body. Bad bacteria, on the other hand, exist in our microbiota as a result of contact with pathogens such as fungi and other disease-causing elements. This happens through the airways and the ingestion of unnatural foods and liquids.

Beneficial and harmful bacteria coexist in the same space, and the battle begins the moment the "good" bacteria have to resist the destruction of the "bad" bacteria. Okay, but what does this have to do with your anxiety? Pretty much everything!

Do you know that feeling of grumpiness, irritability and impatience when the day has barely dawned? It's possible that this is being caused by the decompensation of your intestinal microbiota, which may not be receiving the nutritional support needed to contain the bad bacteria, leaving you at the mercy of their limiting damage and basically responsible for the body's inflammatory state.

To better understand the direct relationship between the gut and anxiety, we need to go back to the anatomy of the brain and its nerve endings. It is in the vagus nerve, which originates in the brain stem, that the connection between the brain and the intestine is made, as this nerve runs along a path from the brain mass to the intestine, connecting it to the central nervous system. Its function is essentially to send vital information from the intestine to the brain and vice versa. This is where the expression "the intestine is the second brain of the human body" comes from.

> The lack of color in your life is directly linked to the lack of color on your plate.

Since physiological and hormonal functions are linked to the gut, your emotions and mood cannot be dissociated from what you eat. Therefore, the lack of color in your life is directly linked to the lack of color on your plate.

Have you ever noticed how your stomach looks in stressful situations? The signs are varied:

- Pain;
- Nausea;
- Burning;
- Tremors;
- Diarrhea;
- Lack of appetite;
- Excessive hunger.

The lack of nutrients, vitamins, minerals and fiber, for example, combined with the continuous stress of everyday life, is the main factor in the imbalance of the chemistry needed to keep us away from the symptoms of anxiety. For this reason, when an imbalance is established, symptoms such as these become more frequent.

So the name we give to the set of microorganisms that live in our body is microbiota. There is an intestinal microbiota, a skin microbiota, a vaginal microbiota and so on. An imbalance in the microbiota is called dysbiosis, which is usually related to a reduction in beneficial microorganisms in contrast to an overgrowth of potentially harmful ones, which contributes to a drop in diversity.

Over the last twenty years, I've been developing strategies to transform people's lifestyles, not just in terms of losing weight, but above all to lead a fully healthy life by transforming their habits as a whole, especially their eating habits. So, if your daily worries have become unbearable and you're still fighting a constant battle against the scale, pay attention to what will be covered later in this chapter, as it will be a decisive step on your path to definitive liberation from the slavery of anxiety.

It is impossible to promote this release without adjusting the intestine, and this is linked to most contemporary diseases. The intestine is made up of millions of cells, but the main role is played by the enterocytes. They are a kind of barrier, which is why they have to be kept together so that nothing harmful can pass through. Imagine ten people hugging each other: that would be the cells of the intestine.

However, some substances and situations can cause the enterocytes to move away, which allows other molecules to cross this barrier, as you can see in the figure below:

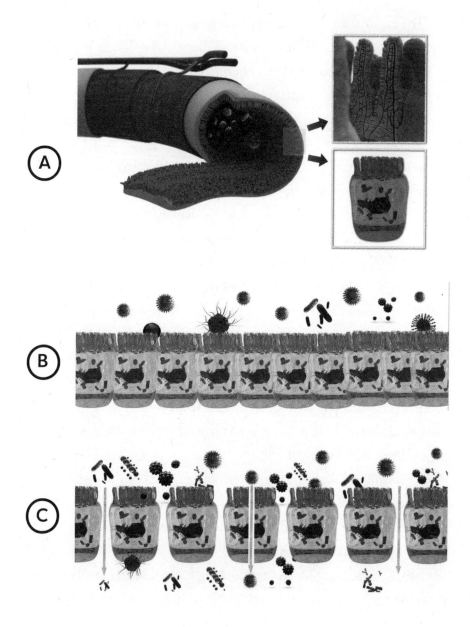

A. INTESTINAL TUBE, VILLI AND ENTEROCYTES;
B. INTACT INTESTINE;
C. LEAKY GUT SYNDROME

Everything you eat is related to the intestinal microbiota. This relationship between the microbiota and the digestive process generates the famous short-chain fatty acids (acetate, propionate and butyrate) and promotes the release of intestinal neuroactivities which, by stimulating certain pathways in the gut, take this information to the brain, impacting eating behavior, cognition, impulsivity, depression and, ultimately, anxiety. So we can't ignore what we eat.

LEAVING NEGATIVE MOODS BEHIND

The main problem when talking about food is that most people insist on associating nutrition, which is so vital to existence, with the term diet, which has gained a rather negative connotation. Just to clarify: there is no such thing as a diet, at least not according to the traditionally presented concept of counting calories, the Moon diet, the Sun diet or any other that conditions the individual to a restricted program limited to a short period.

"AS LONG AS YOU KEEP THINKING YOU'LL BE SAVED BY A MAGICAL DIET, YOU'LL CONTINUE TO BE TIED TO A STUMP LIKE A CIRCUS ELEPHANT."

It's to be expected that the term "diet" will send shivers down the spine of many people, and it's also understandable why adherence to diet programs is so low, at least for long periods of time. This type of practice ends up trapping people in a false sense of control and, worse still, control with a day and time to end. As long as you keep thinking that you'll be saved by a magic diet, you'll continue to be tied down like a circus elephant.

How long will you continue to eat in front of your computer, without a lunch break and without paying attention to what you eat? How long will you continue to eat, while on the move, that greasy snack or any fast, processed food whose shelf life never expires because it's so synthetic?

How long will your life be guided by the drive-thru, balancing between eating fries dripping with oil and sodas full of sugar that will wreak havoc on your gut microbiota?

It is possible to replace the fermentation of your stomach, which can literally eat you up inside and make you sick with anxiety, with the fermentation of natural foods that will not only make you stay alive, but live a full life. To do this, you need to remember that uncontrolled anxiety can destroy your ability to think and, above all, to choose not to live as a slave to your own mouth.

Follow the story below, which tells of the journey from the slavery of anxiety, fueled by binge eating, to the liberation that generates new life. Then think about what your choice will be from now on.

I freed my mind from food slavery

I had thought: "Oh, I don't think I'm going to... I'm going to have to go through a lot of effort and then she'll look me in the face and say: 'Oh, you want to lose weight? Then go on this diet and come back in 30 days'". Who could guarantee that she would get to know me, ask me anything? For someone like me, who has always lived in anxiety, pre-judgment was present in almost every situation. And the anticipated suffering, not to mention.

But when I first heard, about a year and a half ago, that my obesity was due to a lack of nutrition, I almost didn't believe it. "Danielle, you're obese because you don't eat. So you're going to have to learn how to eat and, above all, treat your anxiety before you do anything else." That was the doctor's answer.

In fact, I always went a long time without eating, and when I did eat, I actually tried to eat anything that had sugar in it or that turned into sugar in my body, even though I didn't know it. It had to be sweet, always, and it was only later that I discovered why. In reality, my brain had been addicted to the excitement of the moment for a long time. It was a happiness, a euphoria that came and left me feeling on cloud nine for the first fifteen minutes, as if there were no more problems or loneliness in the world. But after that "high", I felt like crap physically and emotionally. The toxin bomb disguised as sweetness had none of the nutrients I needed, and it also kept me trapped in an endless vicious cycle with food for most of my life.

Although it apparently brought me happiness and silenced my anxiety, compulsive eating actually made me feel like I was taking narcotics. I was really sluggish, to the point of not being able to process ideas, I was always forgetful, sleepy, unwell and moody. Not only did I weigh 120 kilos at 1.65 meters, but the swelling caused by fluid retention was quite painful. So I was even more surprised when I discovered that this process was due to malnutrition as well as dehydration. Since my body didn't know when it would receive any nutrients again, it retained everything in an attempt to keep itself functioning. I had no idea that I was slowly destroying myself.

I know I didn't put on weight overnight, it was a whole process. I never knew how to deal with food without experiencing anguish, and the focus on losing weight was always a part that hurt me a lot. But when I turned 30, the desire to be a mother was stronger than anything I had ever felt. Despite the fear that I wouldn't be able to get pregnant because of my weight, I was aware that changing my eating habits, which I'd spent my whole life avoiding, would be the way to achieve my dream.

I remember when I was 22 years old, I lost 35 kilos in a year. However, I became an even more frustrated, sad and bitter person, because I simply didn't accept the dietary change as a gain in my life, and all I could think about was how torturous diets were. I used to lock myself in my room and wait for my parents to finish their weekend pizza just so I wouldn't have to see that scene. Other times, I'd resort to putting my finger down my throat in a desperate attempt to lose weight.

I was a slave to this situation of putting on weight and losing weight, and as I've always loved beauty and make-up, my focus on the physical was even more pronounced. About three years ago, I started working in a beauty clinic. But shortly afterwards, what seemed like a dream experience turned out to be a real nightmare. Intimidated and depressed by the disapproving looks

I received, I put on even more weight, and it became difficult to swallow the smirks and even the hints about my weight.

But one of the worst days of my life was when I found out that I was the target of fat-phobic attacks from my own supervisor, who referred to me to a stranger as if I were dressed in a gas cylinder cap during an exchange of messages. The pain I felt at that moment because of the offense was the worst humiliation I had ever suffered in my life. It reminded me of the fear I had always felt about my weight and what people could do to me because of it.

However, despite this aggression and the fact that I was psychologically and emotionally shaken for a while, I managed to put an end to the situation. When I told myself that I no longer wanted to live in the past, because getting pregnant in a healthy and conscious way was the most important thing for me, I stopped being on a collision course with food.

Unlike anything I've ever experienced, Dr. Juliano's weight loss program made me see for the first time that my pleasure in eating would be much longer if it came from food that I could peel instead of food that I could take out of a metallic plastic package. With simple substitutions, which I had no idea would be so pleasurable, like drinking green coconut water instead of a carton of juice, I started to feel more and more in the mood, and I no longer felt demotivated, because I was finally taking control of my mind and no longer a slave to the anxiety that always distorted the relationship I had with my body. I learned to define who was in charge of whom within myself.

Now, finally free of the mental control that junk food exerted over me - and that I allowed - I say that it is possible to turn the tables on this desire-food relationship. In addition to quitting my job and opening my own beauty studio, my life is much lighter and more colorful, both on the plate and on a daily basis, and I feel ready to welcome my first child.

Danielle Bernardes, 30, São Paulo.

THE FEAR OF HUMILIATION

Dani's story reveals another of the seven fears we've been discussing throughout this book, the fear of humiliation. This, by the way, comes up a lot when it comes to obesity. When she said that she felt intimidated by other people's stares, Dani had already declared deep down that she was afraid of being judged and humiliated because of the way she looked.

Just as most people feel afraid of being unable to master their own choices when in front of a plate, the fear of embarrassment and shame are limiting feelings. So it's not uncommon for them to seek refuge through taste in order not to face their own pain and, almost automatically, they create obstacles in the vain attempt not to lose something that seems to them to be a lasting source of pleasure.

"Will I be able to eat less?"

"I don't know if I'll be able to do without dessert."

"What's the point of dieting if I have a slow metabolism?"

These and so many other phrases are nothing more than excuses from a mind gripped by the fear of humiliation, which, even before it gets to work to increase the health of the body, triggers messages that fuel the fear of exposure and, consequently, emphasizes the failure of self-control to break out of a vicious cycle established with food in an attempt to overcome humiliation - or even the threat of suffering an eventual humiliation.

With the body's inflammatory levels soaring as a result of the unbalanced microbiota, the now anxious intestine kidnaps the mind, frightened by the realization that it is unable to resist humiliation. This can lead to years, or even a lifetime, of being enslaved by the body itself, which will seek momentary ecstasy in food drugs in order to placate the symptoms of anxiety. It's a real case of anxious feedback.

Perhaps now, just the thought of anxiety taking over your body through the things you eat has triggered an urge to binge on any fatty or sugary junk food. Or you may even be feeling a chill in your stomach or other discomfort, especially if you're not paying attention to how you're fueling yourself.

I know you're probably wondering: "But does this cycle have an end that doesn't culminate in a diet?". The answer is yes, of course there is!

The first thing you need to do is deal with the fear of humiliation. By accepting that you are the only person with real power to dominate your life, freeing yourself from this fear will be a consequence. Furthermore, by having a truly strong motivation, you will be able to overcome any barrier imposed by fear.

DEFLATE AND STRENGTHEN THE BODY

Now that you know the intimate relationship between the gut and the brain and how this connection determines your mood and state of anxiety, the next step will be to deflate your microbiota in order to strengthen your body and mind. To do this, the task will be to feed your good bacteria with vitamins, fiber, minerals, probiotics and prebiotics on a daily basis, consuming foods such as:

1. Active culture yogurt, tempeh, miso, natto, sauerkraut, kefir, Kimchi, kombucha (PROBIOTICS);
2. Beans, oats, bananas, berries, garlic, onions, asparagus, tupinambo and leeks (PREBIOTICS);
3. Vitamins: B9, B12, B1, B6, A and C;
4. Minerals: magnesium, potassium and selenium;
5. Beans, brown rice, berries, oat bran, pears, apples, bananas, broccoli, Brussels sprouts, carrots, artichokes, almonds, walnuts, amaranth, oats (FIBERS).

By incorporating new foods with a high nutritional content, you will notice a gradual improvement in your memory, as well as a slowing down of cognitive decline. In other words, you'll become less and less sluggish in your thinking, more focused and with hormone levels properly regulated for an anxiety-free life.

As well as diversifying your menu with these powerful natural food sources, cutting out harmful agents will be key to winning the battle within yourself. Here's an extra tip: if you want to get rid of night or daytime nightmares, start by cleaning up your insides by avoiding the intake of:

1. Sugar: cakes, cookies, sweets, soft drinks and anything sweetened with sugar or corn syrup with excess fructose;
2. High glycemic index carbohydrates: white bread, white rice, potatoes, pasta and everything made from refined flour;
3. Completely remove gluten from your life: gluten is a protein found in wheat, rye and barley. In other words, no wheat or beer;
4. Artificial sweeteners: aspartame is particularly harmful, but so are saccharin, sucralose

and stevia, which should be consumed in moderate doses and with caution;
5. Fried food: fried potatoes, fried chicken, fried seafood or anything dipped in oil;
6. Bad fats: trans fats, such as margarine, vegetable fat and vegetable oils should be avoided altogether; omega-3 fats, such as vegetable and corn fats; sunflower and safflower fats should be consumed in moderation;
7. Nitrates: an additive used in bacon, salami, sausages and other sausages;
8. Milk and dairy products: milk causes inflammation and is one of the main sources of exomorphins, substances that stimulate the central nervous system and cause addiction.

In order for you to function better and your life to move forward, you need to accept that you are responsible for your own nutrition. Think: which army do you want to feed inside you? The one willing to battle for your most favorable, pleasurable and effective version or the potentially self-destructive one, capable of dissolving you in a pool of anxiety?

When you finally understand that eating only for fun is a sign of addiction that can't fill any emptiness you're feeling, your change of habits will come naturally. Then diet will be just another word, as your life will be much bigger than that. You will exercise dominion over your mind in order to nourish your body in the best style and with no expiration date. As long as, and by now you've probably realized this, you decide not to live like an anxious slave anymore.

MOMENT WITH DR. JU

At this point, I want you to take a closer look at your diet and your bowel habits, because now you've understood the relationship between food, your bowel habits and your emotions.

1. How are your bowel habits in your day-to-day life, does it change with your emotions?

....

....

....

2. Do you have a predilection for any type of food? How do you expect to feel when you eat it?

....
....
....

3. How were you before you ate it??

....
....
....

4. How does what I eat relate to the poop I have?

....
....
....

5. How does what I drink relate to the shape, consistency and frequency of my poop?

....
....
....

CHAPTER 7

THE HOLY REMEDIES AGAINST ANXIETY

> "'I will restore the exhausted and satisfy the weak. Then I woke up and looked around. My sleep had been pleasant."
>
> (Jer 31:25-26)

So far, you've learned that breathing, eating properly and staying hydrated are essential actions in the fight against anxiety. In addition to these, there are other aspects of equal importance, as you will see on the following pages. Your anxiety didn't reach the level it is now overnight and, even though it may come from an isolated factor, the set of symptoms that plague you is not restricted to a single pathway throughout your body.

Now that you've been introduced to the intimate relationship that breathing has with the release of the most common symptoms of anxiety and you know that everything you consume has the power to directly affect your emotional state, it's time to make new reflections and, best of all, new choices.

SLEEP WITHOUT ANXIETY

Have you ever stopped to pay attention to the quality of your sleep?

"Oh, doctor, I don't have the patience to sleep, I think it's a waste of time!"

"Lately, I've been sleeping three or four hours a night. I'm a very light sleeper."

"I have trouble getting to sleep, so I take the opportunity to check my social media when I go to bed."

Although there are many excuses for not getting enough sleep, sleep is just as vital as breathing, eating, drinking and exercising. It is, in fact, the basis for enjoying good health and well-being throughout life.

In the previous chapter, you discovered how the intestinal microbiota is a real powerhouse of your body's functioning which, once out of balance, can leave you in an unwanted state of anxiety. Poor diet isn't the only thing responsible for promoting this imbalance. Inadequate sleep is also strongly linked to recurrent inflammatory bowel diseases.

The immune system relies heavily on sleep to stay healthy. As it is responsible for defending the body against foreign or harmful substances, sleep deprivation can prevent it from strengthening this system, causing the protection of cytokines, which are proteins secreted by defense cells to fight infection, to decline. This means that a person may take longer to recover from illness, as well as anxiety, and may be at an increased risk of contracting chronic diseases.

Inadequate sleep affects the hormones that regulate appetite and increases the risk of obesity. You know that moment when you feel hungrier than when you're well rested? It's the result of an increase in your level of ghrelin, also known as the hunger hormone, which goes through the roof because of sleep deprivation.

In addition, there may be an increased risk of new and advanced respiratory diseases, a risk of type 2 diabetes, due to the release of insulin, which leads to increased fat storage; an increased risk of cardiovascular diseases and problems with the adequate production of hormones, including those linked to growth and testosterone, in the case of men.

* * *

A good night's sleep is incredibly important for your health. Unfortunately, people are sleeping much less than in the past. As if that weren't enough, the quality of sleep has also decreased, due to exposure to increasingly hectic environments full of lights and, in particular, electronic devices, which directly interfere with natural sleep patterns.

In the case of anxious individuals, the scenario is even more complicated. As they usually have unregulated hormone levels and a compromised microbiota, all of this combined with external factors such as situational stress and traumatic events, their sleep is fatally compromised.

Do you remember what we said about inflammation in your body? Inflammatory states are invariably responsible for health problems, which lead to impoverished sleep patterns and are strongly linked to anxiety and depression.

When you exhibit one or more harmful behaviors (disturbances) in your daily sleep, as described below, you may be suffering from sleep deprivation or sleep deficiency. It is important that you observe whether.

- You're getting enough sleep (sleep deprivation);
- Sleep well;
- There are different types of sleep that your body needs;
- Sleeping at the wrong times of the day (out of sync with your body clock);
- You suffer from a sleep disorder that prevents you from getting enough sleep or results in poor quality sleep.

In short, poor sleep can impair your brain function and reduce your social skills, and can even impact your ability to recognize people's emotional expressions, which is directly related to a loss of productivity. Now, if you get good sleep, you have the power to maximize your problem-solving skills, improve your memory and increase your physical and mental performance, which contributes enormously to reducing the symptoms of anxiety.

Sleep helps your brain to function properly. While you sleep, your brain is in full preparation for the next day, forming new pathways to help you learn and remember information. It also prevents possible problems in socializing with other people, irritation, impulsivity and mood swings. It prevents you from feeling sad, depressed or unmotivated, as well as problems with concentration and stress.

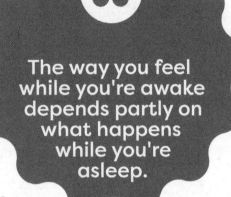

> The way you feel while you're awake depends partly on what happens while you're asleep.

To help you understand sleep deficiency, I'll explain how sleep works and why it's so important. There are two basic types of sleep:

1. Rapid Eye Movement (REM)
2. Non Rapid Eye Movement (NREM)

In these two periods, there is rest through sleep, which can be permeated by dreams, and both usually occur in a regular pattern of three to five cycles each night.

NREM sleep includes what is commonly known as deep sleep or slow-wave sleep. Dreaming, on the other hand, occurs during REM sleep. Your ability to function and feel good while you're awake depends on whether you're getting enough sleep and enjoying enough of each type of sleep. Sleeping at a time when your body is ready is also essential.

Your internal "biological clock" follows a 24-hour repeating rhythm (called a circadian rhythm) that affects every cell, tissue and organ in the body and the way they function. The control of when you are awake and/or when your body is ready to sleep lies with your internal clock. If you're not getting enough sleep, if you're sleeping at the wrong time or if you have poor quality sleep, you'll probably feel very tired during the day. What's more, you may not feel refreshed and alert when you wake up. That's why the way you feel when you're awake depends partly on what happens while you're asleep.

Below, I'll share with you a brief basic manual on what to do to eliminate everything that prevents you from enjoying a good night's sleep, which is a powerful tool against anxiety

POOR SLEEP HYGIENE (THINGS YOU DO THAT IMPAIR YOUR SLEEP)

Some bad habits that affect sleep hygiene and justify this diagnosis are:

- going to bed and getting up at varying times;
- staying in bed for frequent and long periods;
- routinely use products containing alcohol, tobacco or caffeine before going to bed;
- making frequent use of the bed for activities such as watching television, reading, studying and eating;
- exercising close to bedtime;
- engaging in exciting or emotionally disturbing activities too close to bedtime;
- sleeping on an uncomfortable bed, poor quality mattress, inadequate covers, etc;
- allow the bedroom to be excessively bright, stuffy, cluttered, hot, cold or otherwise uninviting to sleep;
- performing activities that require a high level of concentration just before going to bed;

- allow mental activities such as thinking, planning, remembering, etc. to take place in bed.

Establishing and practicing good sleep hygiene can put an end to all these bad habits.

Prevention is the watchword of today's medicine. Most teenagers sleep so well that they believe they can just flop down on the sofa at any time. After the age of 35, however, sleep becomes fragile and requires greater care.

Sleep hygiene rules are there to help you get the most out of your sleep. Unfortunately, they don't work for everyone, especially those at the extremes of age or suffering from sleep disorders or other health problems.

If they don't work for you, write down how you feel and see a doctor so that he can help you identify what can be done.

Poor sleep hygiene is incompatible with maintaining good quality sleep and complete daytime alertness. The complaint of those who take poor care of their sleep can be either insomnia or excessive sleepiness.

PROPER SLEEP HYGIENE (WHAT TO DO TO IMPROVE YOUR SLEEP)

Have a sleep routine with a bedtime and a wake-up time. Do it:

- a tidy room;
- a comfortable mattress and pillows.

Before or at bedtime, AVOID:

- ingest alcoholic beverages, tobacco or caffeine;
- exercising close to bedtime;
- watching TV, messing with your cell phone or working;
- take diuretics (after 6 p.m.) so you don't have to go to the bathroom (talk to your doctor about this).

Search:

- turn off the lights;
- close the curtains;
- check the temperature;
- use aromatizers.

It is now clear that sleep is not just a way of shutting down the brain to rest, but an active, cyclical, complex and changeable state, with profound repercussions on the functioning of the body and mind in the wakefulness of the following day, and one of the main tools in the fight against anxiety.

Sleep is no different from exercise or other states of life. It requires preparation, a suitable environment and a mind free of worries. The advice and recommendations you've just read in this chapter, as well as the following exercises, can help you improve your night-time health and finally achieve anxiety-free sleep.

FASTING AND ANXIETY

Throughout human history, fasting has always represented a turning point in the lives of its followers. Through fasting, it is possible to confront one of the fears that shake individuals, the fear of scarcity, which leads them to think of complete lack, the imminence of need, the absolute absence of resources for survival.

The fear of scarcity is capable of leading you to an excessive search for security, triggered by the worry about lack and its resulting emptiness. This fear is also related to the absence of food. It's no coincidence that facing this fear involves challenging beliefs often established by the people you love the most, through maxims such as "an empty bag won't stand up" or "you have to eat or you'll get sick".

However, despite being seen as a lack, due to the absence of food in its matter, fasting has the power to connect you to something that transcends understanding, allowing you to take a real dive inside. By following the guidelines in this book, fasting becomes another effective tool in the fight against anxiety.

When my wife felt the presence of illness for the first time in her life, she plunged deep into her essence, hearing a call from the depths of her soul inviting her to begin a fast that lasted 21 days. This freed her body and mind and completely manifested her connection in faith with God.

I fasted for 21 days

At no point was I afraid of getting hungry when I started my fasting process. In fact, it didn't even cross my mind, because when I had the screening to see what I had in my breast, even before I received the diagnosis, I felt in my heart that I had to fast. In fact, what I experienced was a spiritual call, because I was very distressed at that moment, and it was as if God said to me: "Daughter, it's time. It's time for total surrender, complete surrender". When I felt that, I just said to Juliano: "I'm going to fast and I don't know how long I'm going to stay, but I need you to support me in this process, because I have to do it; I have to do it". He supported me immediately, as he does in everything, and told me to stick to my purpose.

I started my fasting process with a very firm focus, which was simply to achieve healing through my connection with God, through my fasting. I didn't yet know that I had cancer, because first I needed to deal with some issues in my soul, and it was the healing of my soul that I focused on. For me, illnesses come from the soul, and they end up materializing in the body. I felt that my soul needed that. Fasting was the way to heal my spirit.

However, the very moment I was diagnosed with cancer, I crumbled. I ran out of ground. I remember my husband taking me by the hand, supporting me and welcoming me in the best way he could at that moment. He looked into my eyes and said that he would be with me no matter what. "Don't worry, God is taking care of everything," he told me. And I knew that he was. It was also from then on that I understood even more why I had been called to fast. I understood that this was my first journey of total healing, and it was extremely necessary. I remember looking into the eyes of my children, Caio, the eldest, and Bella, my baby, looking at my husband, my mother-in-law and my brother-in-law, who were at home at the time, and thinking: "Not here. I'm not going to die from this! I determined that I wasn't going to die of cancer, so I cried out to God at that time, just as I cried out to Him throughout the fasting process, asking for strength, asking for focus on what I was doing, and it was incredible.

I only drank water, unsweetened tea and coffee; nothing else. And every time I prayed, every time I asked God for healing, for discernment and for Him to show me the way, persevering during those days of fasting, of that complete spiritual surrender, because I truly threw myself into God's lap, I felt stronger and stronger, more and more nourished! Then the feeling of not eating, of not having food, didn't exist, because I felt extremely refreshed and nourished, I had everything I needed.

God gave me everything I needed during those 21 days. I would wake up and go to sleep with enormous energy. I remember going to do stories and jumping up and down, singing and joking, repeating "13 days of fasting! 13 days of fasting!" and so on throughout the days. And I only finished this process because I had my first chemo and was on a prolonged fast when my first period came after giving birth to my daughter, and that period was hemorrhagic, so I was really weak. So at that point I understood that my body needed to be fed, but as far as I was concerned, I wouldn't stop there.

The whole process of fasting only strengthened me. I remember looking at my breast and joking about the situation, because I faced everything with a lightness that was only possible through faith, God's presence in my life and fasting. I would look at my breast and say: "What's up? Are you starving? Melt! Melt!". I used to say this to the "tutu", which is how I nicknamed the tumor.

It was the best experience I've ever had. I felt a full connection with God, and the certainty that He was taking care of me, that He gives me everything I need, and that everything was already right, as well as the certainty that healing would come.

Carol Pimentel, 38, São Paulo.

> You don't need to and shouldn't do a prolonged fast without your doctor's permission, especially if you are taking medication or have any illnesses. However, it is possible to enjoy fasting in a cyclical and progressive way. Naturally, the freedom of the physical, emotional and spiritual body will manifest itself. Every time we sleep, fasting is already considered. So, if you manage to stop eating at 6 p.m. and only return at 8 a.m. the next day, you will have already fasted for 14 hours.

TIBETAN RITES TO COMBAT ANXIETY

In this battle you've been learning to fight against anxiety from the teachings in this book, victory won't be complete if you don't get your body moving. Physical activity is by far one of the pillars for changing the physiological and behavioral patterns responsible for protecting you from anxiety.

Based on this, one of the practices that I consider to be the most powerful for you to master your anxiety consists of Tibetan rites, a set of physical exercises based on movements created around 2,500 years ago. When combined with deep breathing, they increase blood flow and warm up the muscles. They also improve strength and posture.

These ancient practices became a simplified exercise routine for monks in Tibet and China. The monks were looking for a compact version of postures that would energize the neuroendocrine plexuses, called chakras in the East, which basically function as our body's power boxes, promoting self-healing, strengthening the body and balancing its systems.

The Tibetan rites consist of five yoga postures (asanas) and movements based on improving the body's energy connection through the chakras.

Chakras are not physical. They are the aspects of consciousness that interact with the physical body through two main vehicles: the endocrine system (which controls our hormones) and the nervous system. Each of the seven chakras is associated with one of the seven endocrine glands and a certain group of nerves, called a plexus. The endocrine glands include the pineal, pituitary, ovaries, testes, thyroid, parathyroid, hypothalamus and adrenals.

Thus, each of these chakras can be associated with specific parts of the body, such as the head, throat, chest, stomach, among others, and with specific functions of the body controlled by that plexus or endocrine gland related to that chakra.

Tibetan rites are capable of balancing our hormones, controlling stress and emotions, stimulating the autonomic nervous system and digestion, as well as the resting response, which nourishes our entire body. The postures act directly on the endocrine organs through movements that massage and stimulate organs such as the kidneys, liver and pancreas, stimulating hormone production and flow. Breathing helps the hypothalamus and other glands to balance the endocrine system.

When the seven energy fields are in sync, active and spinning at the same speed, you feel better, more balanced mentally, emotionally and physically.

INCLUDING THE BENEFITS OF TIBETAN RITES IN EVERYDAY LIFE

To start including Tibetan rites in your daily life and enjoy their many benefits, including relief from body pain, especially in the joints, relief from the symptoms of arthritis, improvements in emotional and mental health and a greater sense of well-being and balance, you only need to set aside ten to fifteen minutes of your day. Ideally, each exercise should be repeated 21 times before moving on to the next, but this is a lifelong practice, so there's no need to rush to get to 21 repetitions.

The list of benefits is truly immense, and each practitioner sees improvements in areas of greatest need. After all, the rites work to synchronize energy, and people with depression, anxiety and fear can, through this practice, adjust the chakras and eliminate these symptoms. The important thing is that you start and persist with the exercises in order to reap all the benefits. Pay attention to how your body feels and don't force anything.

During the first week, practice each rite three times a day. Add two repetitions per ritual the following week and keep adding two repetitions per rite each week until you're doing 21 rounds of each rite every day.

THE FIVE TIBETAN RITES:

- Rite 1: Rotation;
- Rite 2: Supine leg raise;
- Rite 3: Knee flexion;
- Rite 4: Team pose at the table;
- Rite 5: Upward and downward dog flow.

It's important to repeat the movements in this sequence to create a cyclical effect on your breathing, emotions and inner being in general.

RITE 1

The first rite is used to stimulate the chakras and contribute to the balance of emotions. It connects energy centers and builds core muscles.

- Stand with your back as straight as possible;
- Extend your arms outwards, parallel to the floor, with your palms facing the floor;
- Staying at the same point, slowly start turning your body clockwise;
- Do not tilt your head forward or backward;
- Keep your eyes open and fixed, looking straight ahead.

RITE 2

This rite strengthens the abdomen and stimulates the energy center associated with your pancreas. If you find it too difficult to perform, you can try bending your knees.

- Start lying on your back with your arms folded at your sides and your palms on the floor;
- Take a deep breath and try to lift your head, simultaneously moving your chin towards your chest;
- Raise your legs, keeping your knees straight;
- Hold this position for as long as you can, then exhale and slowly lower your head and legs to the floor.

RITE 3

This rite is performed to open your solar plexus (system of radiating nerves and ganglia), improve the per-

formance of your heart and throat and also balance your hormones.

- Try to close your eyes while doing this exercise, which will help you concentrate on your breathing.
- Kneel on the floor with your shoulders extended;
- Keep your palms on the back of your thighs, on your buttocks or below them;
- Inhale and arch your spine backwards, which will extend your chest;
- As you exhale, slowly lower your head forward.

RITE 4

The fourth rite has the benefit of strengthening the thigh muscles and improving respiratory capacity.

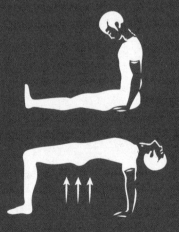

- Sit on the floor with your legs stretched forward and your shoulders extended;
- Place your palms on the floor next to your body;

- Inhale and gently lower your head back, at the same time raising your hips and bending your knees to a table-like position;
- Hold this position for as long as you can. Then exhale and return to the starting position.

RITE 5

According to the ancient Tibetan text, this rite helps revitalize your soul, aids blood circulation and strengthens the muscles in your arms and legs. If you find it difficult to do, you can bend your knee as you move between the positions.

- Stand on the floor with your legs firmly touching the ground;
- Extend your arms upwards and bend your torso, touching the floor with your hands;
- Extend your feet behind you, keeping your shoulders shoulder-width apart. Stretch out your arms and arch your spine, keeping your upper legs on the floor;

- Lower your head into the arch;
- Inhale and lower your hips inwards, moving your body in a "U" shape downwards. Move your chin up towards the sky;
- Exhale and return to the upside-down "V" shape.

Good quality sleep, the practice of fasting and the application of the five Tibetan rites presented in this chapter are invaluable tools in the fight against anxiety. Stop right now and imagine yourself free of the symptoms that are so well known and so unpleasant: insomnia, tachycardia, excessive sweating, nervousness, stress, lack of appetite control, compulsions. Freeing yourself from all of this is entirely possible by making your own choices and facing fears that can't bring you down, given how small you really are.

Choose today to live free from the grip of anxiety by gradually implementing each of the lessons learned in this and the other chapters of this book. I bet you'll soon tell me that it was much easier than you had imagined.

MOMENT WITH DR. JU

Right now, I want you to immerse yourself in the following experiences.

1. How did it feel to apply the Tibetan rites in your daily life, and how do you perceive the implementation of this new habit in your daily life?

....
....
....
....
....

....

....

....

....

....

....

2. At this point I want you to think about how you feel at each fasting time, as shown in the figure on page 192, learning to let go of the sensations and emotions that paralyze you in everyday life and when fasting. Describe what your experience is like in the eating windows and fasting windows:

DIA 1
....

DIA 2
....

DIA 3
....

DIA 4
....

DIA 5
....

DIA 6
....

DIA 7
....

DIA 8
....

DIA 9
....

CHAPTER 8

THE MIRACLE OF LIFE WITHOUT ANXIETY

> "He will wipe away every tear from their eyes. There will be no more death, nor sorrow, nor crying, nor pain, for the old order has passed away."
>
> (Rev 21:4)

Throughout this journey, you have been introduced to anxiety as it originally came into this world and should be: a natural protective reaction of the individual when faced with stimuli that activate their survival instinct. However, what should at first be a normal biological function of the human being has taken on gigantic proportions as a result of its feedback, to the point of becoming one of the main evils of the 21st century.

Fueled by fears, anxiety has taken over minds, bodies and spirits all over the world, triggering a series of disabling symptoms and illnesses.

However, as you have seen, it is possible to put an end to the slavery of anxiety. Starting with the specific activities shared in this book, you can take a deeper look at existence and realize that everything around you that wasn't working for you was really just there to make you stronger.

So, regardless of the degree of anxiety you're facing, it must be made clear that suffering is not a divine punishment, nor is it a force of chance. Each of us is invited every day to look deep within and find our sacred essence, the essence that connects us to the creator who manifests his life throughout the universe.

If your connection is impaired, whether by one of the seven fears or for any other reason, don't worry. To make it easier for you to understand everything we've discussed and to show you how to organize your process of transformation and reconnection with your essence for a life free of anxiety, from now on we'll present you with three fundamental elements that concentrate not only what you've learned so far, but also the foundation on which your freedom will be forged:

- The star of life;
- The death star;
- The star of love.

The star of life is made up of the seven heaths that encompass all areas of our lives. By balancing them, you will achieve full health.

By analyzing the death star, you will be able to recapitulate each of the seven fears previously presented, understanding that each axis interconnects to form the main fear: the fear of death.

However, you will finally discover that you can cast away each of the fears revealed, as well as any fear, through the seven virtues that make up the star of love.

The functioning of the star of life is directly dependent on the star of love, which opposes the star of death. So here's how each of them works so that you can achieve a life of fulfillment and freedom from anxiety.

THE SEVEN HEATHS

All my students follow a precept of building a full life based on the seven healths that involve areas to be worked on daily in their lives, prioritizing the one that most needs to be impacted in the present state. These healths are interconnected, forming the star of life.

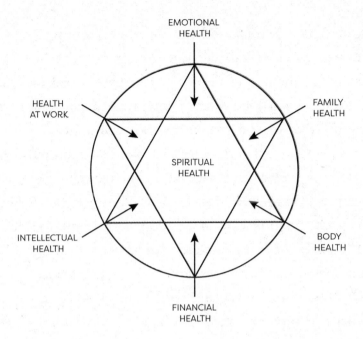

Note that the first health to form this star is emotional health, which is essentially an invitation to take a deep dive into your heart and discover how everything inside you comes out in your daily life. As you begin to truly take care of yourself, ask yourself: How do I respond to emotional situations? Do I need to take a deeper look at this?

Then there's intellectual health. Bear in mind that your brain records everything it's exposed to, so find out how you've been feeding it from everything that's present in your daily life. To understand how you feed your brain, analyze whether you seek continuous improvement, take courses, read books and meet new people. If you're always in the same environment, how can you feed your brain with new information?

Moving on, we come to the health of the body, which has to do with all our functioning systems: circulatory, digestive, hormonal, immune and many others. Therefore, in order to avoid systemic failures, it's vital that you pay attention to how your body is doing, whether it's been strengthened or weakened, and whether you've been doing what your body needs to manifest the health you want. Are you getting the body you want?

The star of life is not just the health of body and mind, because if your pocket is being affected, an imbalance in your financial health will inevitably affect the rest. How are your finances today? What situation in your life do you attribute the health of your finances to? Is it related to your anxiety? And if you had all the money in the world, would you develop new anxiety? To understand how your financial situation relates to others, bear in mind that it is directly linked to how you contribute positively to the lives of others, and how you allow the world to reciprocate this act of service in your life.

Next to emotional health is family health, which shows how you relate to those closest to you, those who love you in essence. Normally, when we're with family, we explode more easily because we know that love in this environment is more tolerant than in the outside world. How is your family? Do you have a solid relationship? How is your relationship with your non-blood family, with those who care about you? Are you able to have someone by your side? Do you allow them to see what's deep in your heart? Are there things that need to be said between you and your spouse? This analysis of how your family health is going is fundamental to checking whether things are in balance and what needs to be looked after.

At the other end of family health is work health, a place that many recognize as their second home - if not their first. If you've never stopped to think about it, now is the time: Do you work with what you love? What is your relationship with what you do? How do you serve others? Are you satisfied with what you receive? What have you done to improve your working environment? What have you done to bring your results closer to your dreams? Many people today are working at something they don't like, for a salary that doesn't satisfy them and, as a result, they find themselves selling their days to make someone else's dream come true.

Finally, we have spiritual health, which is the main one of the seven and encompasses all of them. It determines how you "fight the good fight" on a daily basis. How is your relationship with God? Is there a God? How intimate are you with your beliefs? Do you have a religion? Do you live what you carry in your heart? Are you more concerned with judging than welcoming in love? From the moment you manifest your spiritual health, you will conquer the peace that transcends all understanding.

MAKING THE STAR OF LIFE SHINE

In order to keep your star of life shining brightly, your first task will be to identify which of these healths is most compromised and which, in order of priority, needs to be worked on. Reflect carefully and deeply so that you realize how your fears manifest themselves in each of the healths of your life.

"But doctor, how do I identify the health I need most? Several of them are affected!"

This is one of the most common questions I hear. You should take a deep look at your life and see which of the seven heaths has the greatest impact on your daily pain. The manifestation of anxiety in a woman who has been betrayed, for example, often stems from the disconnection with her husband and the failure to release genuine forgiveness, or to resolve that forgiveness in her life.

> Speaking of forgiveness, do you know when forgiveness really happens? Contrary to what many people think, forgiveness is not forgetting, but being able to remember the fact without it having power over your heart, your emotions, your feelings and your life. Forgiveness is not being complicit with the mistake and living with it again and again. It's getting rid of the hurt you've allowed to settle in your heart because of someone who has hurt you.

Imagine that a sparrow can never affect the existence of an eagle. The planes of existence, the level of perception, the environment, the food, everything is different. Once, during an event, a follower came to me in tears asking for forgiveness after listening to one of my talks, saying that she had meant me harm and had cursed me, among other things. I simply smiled lightly, looked her in the eye and said: "All the evil you've expressed has only existed in your heart. All the energy you've given me is just energy, which can be transformed into whatever I want in my life". I then asked her what had made her feel that way, and she couldn't answer. Then I continued: "You have values that you can't manifest in actions in your life. I don't need to forgive you, I didn't even know who you were until three minutes ago. You have to forgive yourself for not serving in love, but in pain. Wounded people hurt even without realizing it".

"

Every path is an invitation to transcendence, but not everyone is able to perceive transcendence at all times. Forgiveness manifests itself when the fact that led your life to suffering no longer has any power over you or your heart. In this way, your heart lives in peace because it rests eternally in a love that transcends understanding.

"

Some people say that all their anxiety comes from a lack of money. However, I have treated many multimillionaire patients who were anxious. Others say that the cause of their anxiety is worry about their children, parents, work or even the coronavirus pandemic.

We could list thousands of situations for you to justify your limited life in one or more of the seven health areas. The fact is that we are all here to learn continuously and, in reality, our learning curve will only be exponential if we understand that we have the right to constantly learn from our mistakes. We just can't make the same mistakes. Having said that, what is the most important health you need to start working on?

Initially, you need to look at your emotions, your body, your spirituality, the way you connect to work to the detriment of all other health.

How is your intellectual health? How much do you study, read and seek out new information? Just because you're reading this book, your intellectual health already has more points than that of the vast majority of Brazilians.

Learning how to take care of each of these health conditions doesn't have to be through pain if you accept that love is the absolute way to overcome the death star in your life.

LOVE ALWAYS CONQUERS DEATH

Remember how at the beginning of this book I said that in order to beat the enemy called anxiety, you need to know every single detail about it?

You already know that anxiety is basically fueled by fear. So, to highlight each of its faces, meet the death star.

Consisting of the seven main fears that I have observed throughout my career as a health educator for more than 100,000 students in 67 countries, this star, although it exists, does not need to and should not dominate your life.

Throughout each chapter, you get to know all these fears one by one. Through real stories, you can see how the fears of rejection, incapacity, illness, humiliation, scarcity and abandonment can culminate in the darkest of human pains: the fear of death.

You've discovered that "dying of anxiety" is no longer just an expression, but a sad statistic. But you've also learned that you don't have to live a life of terror if you're prepared to disarm the traps of anxiety.

At every moment of this journey I have given you an invitation - a call, in fact. When I insisted that you "breathe", "take a cold shower", "take care of your diet", "take care of your sleep", "move your body", I meant to reveal a secret to you in order to unlock your most powerful force: love.

The star of love, presented below, is the one that should govern your day-to-day life so that the seven healths are in full balance and there is no room for the star of death to destroy your life.

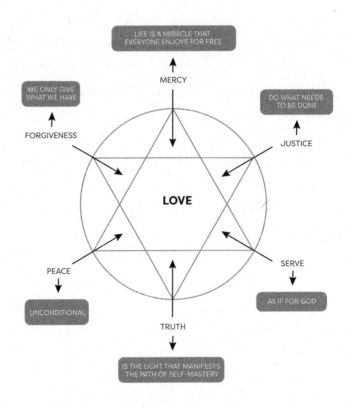

Our star of love begins with mercy. Realize that all of us are only alive within this eternal abundance, this eternal flow that is life, because of mercy. For this reason, when we are completely disconnected from grace, we cannot stand on our own two feet, except through God's mercy, because no matter how much we err, we will always have salvation in the eyes of the Father. Therefore, by thinking that there will always be salvation when your heart is converted, you will receive an air of hope not in man, but in the One who created the whole universe.

On the point of justice, we see that we do what needs to be done. God is just in all his things; creation is all just. Some people talk about action and reaction, but in a straightforward way, if you stop to think about it, the universe is extremely abundant, but to reap the rewards you need to understand the principle of the law of sowing and abundance. Take care of what you plant in your life. Are you sowing in love, justice and forgiveness? Has your sowing borne fruit? By living in this abundant frequency, understanding the principles that govern the Universe and how you should act within this perception, you will then get the answer you need.

Justice lies in doing what needs to be done. You may want financial freedom, for example. So what do you need to do to achieve that freedom? Or you may want peace of mind, in which case, what do you need to do to achieve it? When you look at yourself, what do you have to give up? What do you have to do, which people do you have to follow? Who or what do you have to look for? Think about it.

When we come to serve, we enter into a movement of acting for others, and within this action we manifest love. If at that moment we act as if it were for God, for what we value most, we give ourselves and serve in the best possible way, whether it's for others or for ourselves. And this, contrary to what some might think, doesn't hold us back, but drives us forward. Based on this, observe whether what you have been doing in your life is the fruit of genuine love. If not, the lack of impetus for your growth could become a constant in your day.

In order to live a light, full and fear-free life, we need to carry a light heart, which is only possible through forgiveness, which goes hand in hand with mercy. In forgiveness, we recognize the other person's limitation on us. But if we hold any kind of grudge against the other person, this causes us to live in fear of that happening again, or keeps us in a relationship of pain and regret with that other person, which also limits our existence, leading us once again to fear. Can you see how the biggest cause of anxiety feeds back?

The state of unconditional peace is only achieved when we feel loved, because true love casts out all fear. This peace, which transcends all understanding, comes in the presence of the also transcendental welcome, the one that involves us in what goes beyond what we understand, know and perceive. It's that moment when everyone says: "But how is so-and-so standing?". He's standing because what keeps him standing comes from beyond him, it comes through mercy, peace, the improbable, and so the truth manifests itself.

Finally, we come to the other end of the star of love: the truth. When we face the truth, we encounter things as they are. There is no such thing as fear, because fear is only a creation of the mind. There is actually a fact in our relationship with it, regardless of the pain or pleasure it brings, and when we are exposed to the truth, we manifest a path that demands self-mastery. It is within this self-mastery that we achieve liberation and full connection in love.

MOMENTO COM O DR. JU

Welcome to the last moment with Dr. Ju in this book! I invite you to access this QR Code and see the message I recorded especially for you before you answer the last questions below.

1. Have you ever been in a situation where it was difficult to calm down? How did it happen? How long did it go on for? How often does it happen in your life?

2. Do you always feel nervous? How does this happen? How long does this state last? How often does this happen in your life?

3. Have you ever worried about situations in which you might panic and look ridiculous? How did this happen? How long did it go on for? How often does it happen in your life?

4. Have you ever found it difficult to relax? How did this happen? How long did it last? How often does it happen in your life?

"A fact that needs to be understood is that love casts out all fear, and every cycle of pain only ends with love. So, from the moment you accept in love each of the changes proposed here, your life will finally be free from the bondage of anxiety."

EPILOGUE

THE ANSWER TO WHAT FOR

> "Love one another as I have loved you. Only then will you be recognized as my disciples,"
>
> (Jn 13:34-35)

At the beginning of this book, I shared the story of my wife Carol's discovery of breast cancer shortly after the birth of our daughter. But the battle to fight the seven-centimeter tumor that had reached her left breast wouldn't be the only one to be fought, as during her cancer treatment Carol also suffered from a new condition called Petersen's hernia, which is a complication of bariatric surgery. The chemotherapy treatment hadn't finished yet and my wife was rushed to hospital and had to undergo emergency surgery.

At the beginning of this book, I shared the story of my wife Carol's discovery of breast cancer shortly after the birth of our daughter. But the battle to fight the seven-centimeter tumor that had reached her left breast wouldn't be the only one to be fought, as during her cancer treatment Carol also suffered from a new condition called Petersen's hernia, which is a complication of bariatric surgery. The chemotherapy treatment hadn't finished yet and my wife was rushed to hospital and had to undergo emergency surgery.

As I've already shared with you, one of the greatest fears of human beings, if not the greatest, is the fear of death, and it was there, at that moment, that Carol faced this fear, because she had to stop chemotherapy, to which she was responding well, then ended up in the ICU, and then underwent not just one, but two emergency abdominal surgeries for intestinal obstruction. The first time it all happened, we left our home in the interior of São Paulo for the capital in the middle of the night, her sedated in the car, and when we arrived at the emergency room Carol was already in a pre-infarction state due to a hydroelectrolytic imbalance caused by low potassium in her blood. She was in a state of intestinal loop distress, and her condition stabilized very slowly, so that she only underwent surgery after midnight on what seemed like an endless day.

Even though she was facing cancer, which was discovered shortly after giving birth, my wife underwent abdominal surgery, but the feeling of relief lasted almost no time, because as soon as she was discharged and we left the hospital, we were back there in less than ten hours due to a new intestinal obstruction. Carol returns to the operating room and undergoes a second abdominal surgery.

In total, she spent 21 days in hospital. During all those days in the ICU, she arrived at her extreme low weight, having to receive three blood transfusions and endure all the complexities of her recovery while still an oncology patient. That moment was marked by her greatest fear of dying. As she made her way from the ICU to the operating room, I remember her saying: "Father, into your hands I commit my life. Do whatever you want". Then she looked at me and said: "Be with me in surgery praying, love, because I've already given my life to God".

* * *

Prayer of St. Francis
Sir,
Make me an instrument of your Peace.
Where there is Hate, may I bring Love,
Where there is offense, may I bring forgiveness.
Where there is discord, may I bring unity.
Where there is doubt, may I bring faith.
Where there is Error, may I bring Truth.
Where there is despair, may I bring hope.
Where there is Sadness, may I bring Joy.
Where there is darkness, may I bring light!
Master,
make me look for more:
to console, than to be consoled;
to understand than to be understood;
to love than to be loved.
For it is by giving that one receives.

By forgiving, you are forgiven and
it is by dying that one lives for eternal life!
Amen

* * *

The best way to understand death is to die to your fears, and it is by dying that you live for eternal life. When we die to our fears, the fear of death only vanishes when you have a state of full presence in connection with God.

After winning the battle against intestinal obstructions, Carol returned to the operating table for the third time, this time to face mastectomy. And because she had stopped chemotherapy - she still had two chemo sessions before her hospitalization due to the hernia she had suffered - her own doctor no longer believed it would be possible to fight the tumor with treatment, as it was still oscillating between two and two and a half centimeters in size. Everyone believed that she had arrived for abdominal surgery with the tumor still in her breast, and at the time no imaging tests were repeated after surgery. So what happens when Carol returns to the hospital and the mastectomy procedure begins? There were no more cancer cells present.

When she came out of sedation and I told her that there was no more tumor, Carol realized that the whole journey, regardless of how it had been, had been worth it, because the way we had welcomed each event, doing everything possible within the realms of medicine and spirituality, it was as if we had received everything as a gift. The miracle had finally been achieved.

That's how we finally had our "what for" answer. After all, for Carol to awaken, she had to go through this whole journey of healing and deliverance. In order for her to awaken in faith and intimacy with God, for us to work in communion within our family while facing a deadly illness, and for us to help thousands of people from the moment we decided to expose the whole process we were going through to the world, going through the turbulence with love and lightness, and showing people that it is possible to survive all this without getting lost along the way, we had to die to our fears in order to truly understand what unconditional love was and thus live eternal life.

* * *

When we experience unconditional love, we are able to have in our lives the manifestation of service, truth, mercy, forgiveness, justice and peace that transcends understanding.

Now, imagine every area of the full life being created on the basis of this kind of energy that permeates us all. We reach a path that manifests the truth for what it is, through self-mastery, the mastery of one's own heart. Now you know which essence to manifest in your being and where to start.

The whole journey we've traced so far now opens up the clearing you needed to see yourself and then take your own steps towards a life without the burden of anxiety. I hope you've enjoyed this journey, and if you'd like to go deeper into the subject, come and join our courses.

A kiss on the heart and a hug on the soul!

IMPORTANT NOTE:
FINAL SURPRISE!

Check out this latest video I've recorded especially for you to consolidate all the achievements you've made so far.

REFERENCES

Berthelot E, Etchecopar-Etchart D, Thellier D, Lancon C, Boyer L, Fond G. Fasting Interventions for Stress, Anxiety and Depressive Symptoms: A Systematic Review and Meta-Analysis. *Nutrients*. 2021 Nov 5;13(11):3947. doi: 10.3390/nu13113947. PMID: 34836202; PMCID: PMC8624477.

Brown RP, Gerbarg PL. Yoga breathing, meditation, and longevity. *Ann N Y Acad Sci*. 2009 Aug;1172:54-62. doi: 10.1111/j.1749-6632.2009.04394.x. PMID: 19735239.

Buijze GA, Sierevelt IN, van der Heijden BC, Dijkgraaf MG, Frings-Dresen MH. The Effect of Cold Showering on Health and Work: A Randomized Controlled Trial. *PLoS One*. 2016 Sep 15;11(9):e0161749. doi: 10.1371/journal.pone.0161749. Erratum in: PLoS One. 2018 Aug 2;13(8):e0201978. PMID: 27631616; PMCID: PMC5025014.

Campanelli S, Tort ABL, Lobão-Soares B. Pranayamas and Their Neurophysiological Effects. *Int J Yoga*. 2020 Sep-Dec;13(3):183-192. doi: 10.4103/ijoy.IJOY_91_19. Epub 2020 Sep 13. PMID: 33343147; PMCID: PMC7735501.

Foster JA, McVey Neufeld KA. Gut-brain axis: how the microbiome influences anxiety and depression. *Trends Neurosci*. 2013 May;36(5):305-12. doi: 10.1016/j.tins.2013.01.005. Epub 2013 Feb 4. PMID: 23384445.

Govindaraj R, Karmani S, Varambally S, Gangadhar BN. Yoga and physical exercise – a review and comparison. *Int Rev Psychiatry*. 2016 Jun;28(3):242-53. doi: 10.3109/09540261.2016.1160878. Epub 2016 Apr 4. PMID: 27044898.

Gudden J, Arias Vasquez A, Bloemendaal M. The Effects of Intermittent Fasting on Brain and Cognitive Function. *Nutrients*. 2021 Sep 10;13(9):3166. doi: 10.3390/nu13093166. PMID: 34579042; PMCID: PMC8470960.

Hamm AO. Fear, anxiety, and their disorders from the perspective of psychophysiology. *Psychophysiology*. 2020 Feb;57(2):e13474. doi: 10.1111/psyp.13474. Epub 2019 Sep 16. PMID: 31529522.

Jayawardena R, Ranasinghe P, Ranawaka H, Gamage N, Dissanayake D, Misra A. Exploring the Therapeutic Benefits of Pranayama (Yogic Breathing): A Systematic Review. *Int J Yoga*. 2020 May-Aug;13(2):99-110. doi: 10.4103/ijoy.IJOY_37_19. Epub 2020 May 1. PMID: 32669763; PMCID: PMC7336946.

Lessan N, Ali T. Energy Metabolism and Intermittent Fasting: The Ramadan Perspective. *Nutrients*. 2019 May 27;11(5):1192. doi: 10.3390/nu11051192. PMID: 31137899; PMCID: PMC6566767.

Méchin O. Angoisse, peur et panique en temps de crise sanitaire [Anxiety, fear and panic in the time of a health crisis]. *Soins*. 2021 Jun;66(856):49-52. French. doi: 10.1016/S0038-0814(21)00165-1. PMID: 34187656.

Oei TP, Sawang S, Goh YW, Mukhtar F. Using the Depression Anxiety Stress Scale 21 (DASS-21) across cultures. *Int J Psychol*. 2013;48(6):1018-29. doi: 10.1080/00207594.2012.755535. Epub 2013 Feb 21. PMID: 23425257.

Peirce JM, Alviña K. The role of inflammation and the gut microbiome in depression and anxiety. *J Neurosci Res*. 2019 Oct;97(10):1223-1241. doi: 10.1002/jnr.24476. Epub 2019 May 29. PMID: 31144383.

Shi L, Deng J, Chen S, Que J, Sun Y, Wang Z, Guo X, Han Y, Zhou Y, Zhang X, Xie W, Lin X, Shi J, Lu L. Fasting enhances extinction retention and prevents the return of fear in humans. *Transl Psychiatry*. 2018 Oct 9;8(1):214. doi: 10.1038/s41398-018-0260-1. PMID: 30301955; PMCID: PMC6177454.

Simpson CA, Diaz-Arteche C, Eliby D, Schwartz OS, Simmons JG, Cowan CSM. The gut microbiota in anxiety and depression

A systematic review. *Clin Psychol Rev.* 2021 Feb; 83:101943. doi: 10.1016/j.cpr.2020.101943. Epub 2020 Oct 29. PMID: 33271426.

Tinsley GM, La Bounty PM. Effects of intermittent fasting on body composition and clinical health markers in humans. *Nutr Rev.* 2015 Oct;73(10):661-74. doi: 10.1093/nutrit/nuv041. Epub 2015 Sep 15. PMID: 26374764.

Tovote P, Fadok JP, Lüthi A. Neuronal circuits for fear and anxiety. *Nat Rev Neurosci.* 2015 Jun;16(6):317-31. doi: 10.1038/nrn3945. Erratum in: Nat Rev Neurosci. 2015 Jul;16(7):439. PMID: 25991441.

Van de Wouw, M., Schellekens, H., Dinan, T. G., & Cryan, J. F. (2017). Microbiota-Gut-Brain Axis: Modulator of Host Metabolism and Appetite. *The Journal of Nutrition*, 147(5), 727–745. doi:10.3945/jn.116.240481

Verma D, Wood J, Lach G, Herzog H, Sperk G, Tasan R. Hunger Promotes Fear Extinction by Activation of an Amygdala Microcircuit. *Neuropsychopharmacology.* 2016 Jan;41(2):431-9. doi: 10.1038/npp.2015.163. Epub 2015 Jun 11. PMID: 26062787; PMCID: PMC4579557.

Wong ML, Inserra A, Lewis MD, Mastronardi CA, Leong L, Choo J, Kentish S, Xie P, Morrison M, Wesselingh SL, Rogers GB, Licinio J. Inflammasome signaling affects anxiety – and depressive-like behavior and gut microbiome composition. *Mol Psychiatry.* 2016 Jun;21(6):797-805. doi: 10.1038/mp.2016.46. Epub 2016 Apr 19. PMID: 27090302; PMCID: PMC4879188.

BOOKS TO CHANGE THE WORLD. YOUR WORLD.

To find out about our upcoming releases and available titles, visit:

🌐 www.**citadel**.com.br

f /**citadeleditora**

📷 @**citadeleditora**

🐦 @**citadeleditora**

▶ Citadel – Grupo Editorial

For more information or questions about the work, please contact us by email:

✉ contato@**citadel**.com.br